RAP SHEET

INSIDE THE LIFE OF A CAREER CRIMINAL

Jane,
Mark 11:24
Phil Ham

Phil Hamman & Sandy Hamman

Sandy Hamman
—Many blessings!
11-9-17

eLectio Publishing

Little Elm, TX

Rap Sheet: Inside the Life of a Career Criminal
By Phil Hamman & Sandy Hamman

ISBN-13: 978-1-63213-436-3
Published by eLectio Publishing, LLC
Little Elm, Texas
http://www.eLectioPublishing.com

5 4 3 2 1 eLP 21 20 19 18 17

Printed in the United States of America.

The eLectio Publishing creative team is comprised of: Kaitlyn Campbell, Emily Certain, Lori Draft, Court Dudek, Jim Eccles, Sheldon James, and Christine LePorte.

Publisher's Note
The publisher does not have any control over and does not assume any responsibility for author or third-party websites or their content.

Dedicated to all those who never gave up hope on someone whose life seemed hopeless. To those who've spent sleepless nights and shed tears for someone on the wrong path. For those who kept the faith that change was possible. You made our world a better place.

Thank you to Kim Gulbranson, Marci Risner, and Amy Schmidt for your diligent editing, support, and input. We are grateful to the eLectio team for their tireless work in bringing our stories to print.

CONTENTS

Prologue

Have you ever put up so many walls between you and the world that you can no longer see outside? You put them there for protection, of course. You built some for privacy; to get a little peace and quiet once in a while. Okay, maybe you didn't want anyone to see what you were up to. But some are there to keep out the enemies, and God knows you can't help but acquire some of those over the years; people are idiots. Reluctantly you placed some boundaries for those do-gooders who insisted they're only trying to save you from yourself. And now this grand fortress you proudly constructed has so many barricades and blockades that it's more of an endless maze, and you've lost your way. So here you sit in a prison of your own making so that even when you're out of prison, you're really not.

—Matt Lofton

I stood in the foyer of the Minnehaha County Jail squinting beneath the buzz of fluorescent lights that hung low in the aged quartz block building. Standing alone in the eerie late-night quiet made it feel as if I were in a medieval dungeon. Naturally impatient, I shuffled my feet and watched while the clock's second hand completed yet another rotation. It was 11:30 PM and half an hour had already passed since I'd scribbled in the blanks on some paperwork and handed a bored turnkey the necessary Benjamins to bail my bro Matt out of the pokey. It was when I wiped the last of the sweat from my adrenaline high off my temples and onto my pants that I saw the drops of crimson blood splattered on my blue jeans and boots. It was all that remained from the violent street fight that had landed Matt here again. The combination of whiskey and what I deemed unnecessary delay got my temper flaring; it was an undesirable trait I shared with Matt. The night was young, and time was ticking.

Finally a cell door clanked in the distance; that familiar sound of incarceration. And there he was, coming down the hallway with the Matthew swagger that was more of a glide than a walk that carried his athletic 6'1", 215-pound frame. Considering the events of the night, Matt was clearly unfazed as shown by the kid-like glee in his steel-blue eyes. They were big eyes, too, headlights that had earned him the nickname "Owl" since he did most of his activities in the darkest part of the night.

"I knew you'd be here to get me." Matt beamed, slapping a forceful bear hug around my body. We walked out into the muggy August air elated at not having our entire evening marred by the cops. Our high spirits lasted about two hours, at which point Matt got arrested a second time, a small feat yet one we retold with awe for years to come. But that was Matthew.

—Phil Hamman, co-author

It was hard for me to decide whether Matt had a tangible magnetism or a cultlike lure; an enviable self-confidence or a self-centeredness bordering on narcissism. To my surprise, he was well read and could converse on almost any topic, including the multifaceted Reaganomics we'd recently debated. Me, a college econ major who memorized some facts and attempted a battle of wits with Matt, who'd analyzed each angle of this philosophy with a maturity that comes from having experienced life's harsher lessons.

Without a doubt he was unpredictable and explosive. When my sister sat next to him in middle school, she developed an immediate fear of this complex person. When I was dating Phil and he was off with Matt, I worried. A phone call late at night meant bad news.

But then Matthew would be gone again, incarcerated, only to reappear in our lives like that proverbial bad penny. Matt lived a life on the edge while I played it safe, so his was an enthralling life shrouded in mystery. Phil eventually parted ways with this extreme lifestyle, but Matt's life remained derailed, and I considered him eternally lost. His return would have been no less astonishing had he returned from the dead, which some may say he did.

—Sandy Hamman, co-author

Authors' Note

Doctors use the term antisocial personality disorder (ASPD) to describe what the layman generally refers to as a psychopath (someone without a conscience) or sociopath (someone with a weak conscience). Those with ASPD show a disregard for the rights of others and may have a superficial charm or a tendency to be irritable and aggressive. They are irresponsible and tend to enjoy high-risk activities, disregard laws, and act impulsively. They care only about their own survival and will use any means to attain their goals. The big question is whether this is willful behavior, nature, or nurture. Can people with ASPD be cured? It is one of the most difficult personality disorders to treat, primarily since the subjects have little interest in changing. A few specialists even theorize that excessively altruistic people and sociopaths are two beings from the same branch; both suffer from extremes in their personalities. If the sociopath's conscience were developed, he or she might instead be overly helpful and generous.

Chapter 1
Indoctrination

Matt was so close to earning Henry's favor, even though there was no evidence that this ringleader had ever shown favor to anyone. Matt felt it last month when Henry had possibly looked down on him with approval. Ever since then he'd worked hard to perfect his craft. In fact, Matt could now walk without making a sound. It didn't matter whether he was crossing a squeaky floor or a gravel lot. He moved as though buoyed by some unseen spirit, yet at this moment he was more concerned that he might be seen than heard. And with his dishwater blond hair and too-pale skin in this part of the city, he may as well have announced his presence with fireworks, though the predawn darkness made for good cover. A thundering rain in the middle of the night left a fresh, earthy scent that Matt briefly noticed and inhaled before wiping away water droplets from the glass with his sleeve. He cupped both hands over his eyes and pressed his face against the driver's side window. *Nope. Not this one.* His giftedness as a quick study had made him a natural on the street; he observed as long as necessary, but then his bold nature soon had him taking charge. It made him the perfect accomplice for Henry, who would be expecting the goods to be delivered soon. Matt wandered on to the next car and pulled up the hood of his jacket, more to ward off the gusty spring wind that was whipping trash down the street than to hide his identity.

His brother, Dan, who claimed to never feel anxiety on these outings, wore a secondhand sweatshirt and carried the necessary

1

cooking pot. The fear of being caught didn't faze him. "Hurry up, dork." Dan scowled and scraped the chipped handle of the cooking pot across the fender of a sedan, a senseless act born of hatred that didn't go unnoticed by Matt.

This side street in a shabby section of Springfield, Illinois, was mostly deserted at this hour. Matt strolled along confidently. If anyone asked what he and Dan were doing, they'd claim to be headed to a friend's. But no one ever asked. A dark Continental weaved down the street and then chugged to a stop halfway up on the curb. Five people spilled from the car shrieking with laughter that swept down the otherwise silent street. None of them noticed the two brothers half a block away, hiding in the shadows and waiting for the group to leave so they could continue down the street.

"That was some quick thinkin' for someone with such a thick head!" one of the revelers shouted, which caused the others to fall into raucous laughter.

"Yeah, this little guy here almost got his first taste of jail," another one said, patting the shortest one firmly on the head.

Judging by the littlest one's size, Matt guessed the kid was in junior high, which got him thinking: *When is someone too young to go to jail?* The partiers disappeared into a house and Matt hustled to catch up with Dan. He trailed behind his brother, searching for another car to steal. This was how they spent their Saturday mornings. Dan, being three years older, took the lead in whatever they did, and Matt followed, taking careful mental notes. Both kept an ear open for approaching cars, yet they failed to notice an older teenager with curly, ebony hair standing in the predawn shadows of an adjacent yard holding a baseball bat. It was little slip-ups like this that could lead to fights, beatings, or even death in this neighborhood. Matt saw the boy just in time and caught himself before making the mistake of looking startled. He'd lived in places like this long enough to know that showing fear branded you as a target, a coward. Without saying a word to each other, Matt and

Dan moved to the end of the block, turned the corner, and took off at a full run before reaching a safe distance a few blocks away.

"Think he was going somewhere to play baseball?" Matt looked around to make sure there were no more unexpected visitors hovering around.

Dan shrugged and ran a hand over the now closely cropped bristles atop his head. "Who cares? We could take him out." They had moved here only a few months ago from a harsh Chicago neighborhood, and Dan understood the importance of the tough-guy attitude. He was cocky, confident, and assumed a painted on half-smirk in his best attempt to look indifferent. Combined with a cowlick that forced him to adopt a side part, he resembled a handsome '50s greaser.

He wanted to have his long hair back, but their stepdad, Tom, would have none of that, frequently pulling at a tuft of their hair and smirking that it was time to "chop their mop" again. While others had begun growing long hair to protest the Vietnam War, Tom still embraced the conventional thinking of the 1950s and insisted Matt and Dan wouldn't be seen looking like ragtag hippies.

They hustled down the street. It didn't usually take this long to find an easy mark, and the horizon was turning pink. It would not be a good idea to disappoint Henry considering the protection he offered. When the sound of a car coming down the street grew louder, the two moved together and leaned back against a parked car, arms crossed, looking over their shoulders as if waiting for someone, until the vehicle passed. Dan, who crossed to the other side of the street, finally yelled over to Matt.

"This punk left the ignition in the unlocked position. Keep watch. I'll see if she'll fire up." He felt no pity for anyone who'd leave such an easy mark, and in fact, he'd be doing the idiot a favor by teaching him a valuable lesson.

Matt felt uneasy when Dan talked louder than necessary. *The moron doesn't need to draw attention to us like that.* Matt was naturally more catlike and stealthy with a fervid sensitivity to his

3

surroundings, a good attribute in these parts. He kept watch, scanning the street, while Dan climbed into the old Chevy. The car had a flint lock ignition that could be turned to the starting position if the switch had not been rotated to the locked setting. Dan pulled Tom's screwdriver from his back pocket, inserted the tip, and turned the ignition to the starting position. The thrill of the heist made Matt's blood tingle. The car sparked to life as did Matt, and the brothers were soon careening down the street.

Dan laughed suddenly and gave Matt a brotherly punch to the shoulder. "Let's go to school, fool."

Matt leaned back into the passenger's seat and threw Dan a scowl. The first light of dawn was peeking above the horizon. Neither of the boys was eager to go to school during the week, much less on the weekend. School, for now anyway, was St. Patrick Catholic School where their mother, Mary, had enrolled them hoping to put the fear of God into her boys. So far it hadn't worked. Matt didn't start an argument though. Dan was driving, and Matt knew he used any opportunity to be the boss. With one quick lane change and a sharp right down a side street, they ended up in the narrow driveway that led to the school parking lot now littered with the night's empty beer cans and cigarette butts. St. Patrick sat just off of a main avenue but was L-shaped and had only the empty parish to one side, so the boys headed to a secluded section of the schoolyard where the city noises and yips of alert dogs faded to the background.

Dan's eyes fluttered before he suddenly reached down and picked up a baseball-sized rock. Matt had never thought of his brother as small until now, but a vexed life had taught him to notice the little things. Dan's mouth twitched and a nervous Adam's apple bounced like the bobber on a fishing line; his clenched jaw quivered, his face twisted with rage, and without warning, he pitched the rock through a classroom window. "THAT ONE'S FOR THE FATHER!" he yelled with bulging neck veins. He hurled a second rock. "THAT ONE'S FOR THE POPE!" Another window shattered with a *crack*. Matt shrugged and joined in, while window

4

after window fell victim to their destruction. Within minutes, piles of glass shards shone faintly in the weak light, and Dan continued his rampage, growing louder and angrier with each throw. As usual, Matt was wary. Instinctively, his darting eyes caught the police car making a U-turn down the road and heading toward the parking lot.

"Let's go!" Matt thumped Dan on the back. Matt's confidence crumbled at the sight of the black-and-white car racing toward them.

Dan yanked the car into drive, roared over the sidewalk, bounced off the curb, and hightailed it down a side street with the tires squealing, but the police car was right on them with flashing red lights and screaming sirens. Dan pressed the gas pedal to the floor and looked at Matt with eyes that had grown round. *Don't give up without a fight* was the motto around their neighborhood. Buildings whizzed past in a blur. Ahead, two kids stepped off the curb and onto the street. Dan swerved, and the kids jumped backward just in time. When he crossed two lanes of traffic and squealed around a corner, Matt grabbed onto the door handle for support just before they nearly sideswiped a parked truck. The police car pressed in on them. Then Dan missed a curve and went careening into a deep ditch which sent their heads hurling into the dash with a sickening thud. A gush of warm blood poured down Matt's face and onto his clothes. The blaring sirens closed in on them, and car doors slammed.

"PUT YOUR HANDS UP! HANDS UP!" Traffic slowed at the sight of the spectacle, and a voice crackled from the squad car radio.

With his .38 drawn, a veteran officer cautiously approached the smoking car. "Leave your hands where—" His outstretched arm fell to his side. "What the hell?" He made eye contact with Matt, who was looking back at him through the rearview mirror, walked closer, and put the gun back in the holster. Matt watched the officer's look of intensity fade to disbelief. "Hey, you're not gonna believe this," he called over his shoulder to his partner.

5

With hands cuffed behind their backs, the boys were transported to the jail and placed in a holding cell where they sat on a cold, steel bench, Matt swinging his feet back and forth, staring through the cell bars until Mary, their mom, arrived. Even with the racket of unruly inmates in the background, he remained unnerved knowing she'd swear a blue streak at him, demand to know what his problem was, and then with a shrug, the whole incident would blow over. Later that night she might even feel so bad about yelling that she'd present each of them with one of the coveted pop-top cans of pudding reserved for special occasions.

With a clang of the door, an officer ushered the boys into the front office where Mary stood next to the sergeant's desk, one hand on her hip, punctuating each sentence with reminders to the boys that "The devil has you! You know that, don't you?" She swore, puffed on a cig, and gave the boys her best wait-until-I-get-you-home look. Throughout this verbal hit-smack, the sergeant behind the desk kept up his futile attempts to explain to her what had transpired before tossing his hands in the air and releasing the boys into her custody. With a scowl of defeat, he pushed a large, black pot over to her. "By the way, here's your cooking pot. We found it in the stolen vehicle." Dan used it to sit on so he could see over the steering wheel. He was twelve, and Matt had just turned nine. Already, they were headed down a road of crime and destruction.

Chapter 2
Mother Mary

Mary Barr, the boys' mother, had grown up in the safety of historic Carlinville, Illinois, with an older sister she adored. If her family had chosen one word to describe her, it would have been *wild*. Mary preferred the term *independent*. She'd barely turned twenty when she and a girlfriend pulled their hair into high ponytails, tied them with flimsy scarves, and hopped a train to experience the thrill of the big city they'd both read about in *Life* magazine but had never experienced. Mary craved a more interesting life than what she could find as one of the small fish in elitist Carlinville. Karma brought her to a bar in Chicago where a truck driver named Al Lofton swept her off her feet and within weeks asked her to marry him. Mary couldn't refuse this offer, an opportunity to escape the rejection she'd felt all her life back in the hometown where she'd never quite fit.

This fast-paced marriage lasted just long enough to produce two boys in three years, Dan and Matt. She thrived on the occasional nights out on the town with Al, where she could enjoy a few drinks and share raucous laughs without the prying eyes of small-town neighbors looking on. Even as a young mother, she was carefree and enjoyed speaking her mind and philosophizing with others. Al seemed to enjoy it, too. At first.

He had a less savory side that he'd saved until the girl was officially his. He wore a happy façade out in public but discarded it

7

at the front door of their house before stepping inside. He drove a semi truck, and after returning from several days on the road, the drinking started. Heavy drinking. She dreamed of turning him into one of the gallant heroes she'd read about in fast-paced Harlequin novels, but Al was no bodice-ripping-Linc-Forrester-romance-hero who desired nothing more than to be at the beck and call of his woman. Instead, he became a listless drunk with no interest in having a family. And one day, when Matt was four and Dan seven, Al returned to an empty house.

Alone and raising the boys on her own, Mary worked tirelessly at a variety of jobs to keep a roof over their heads and food on the table. Al didn't contribute even a dime, which made Mary even more determined to prove to him and the folks back home that she didn't need anyone's help. No matter what she had to do. At the time she had no way of realizing the drastic decisions she'd eventually make to keep her family together. Besides, she was lonely, insecure, and had her hands full with two difficult boys. She'd gone to beauty school years before, but her license had lapsed, so before leaving Al, she'd secured a job as a waitress at a local cafe and worked every shift to support the three of them. She loved meeting new customers and spending weekends with her friends letting their hair down. Her ability to see the good in people, even when they didn't recognize it in themselves, was both a gift and ultimately a curse on them all. She understood people, perhaps too well at times, and teetered between being convincing and downright intimidating, especially if it came to meeting the needs of her boys or customers who supplied her wages.

The pleasant aromas of sizzling burgers and fresh coffee met the loyal patrons at the corner café where Tom was a fry cook and Mary a waitress. She had fallen for him before she'd had time to grab her first order pad. She knew the feeling was mutual once she realized she could squeeze favors from him where the other waitresses couldn't. Where they saw an arrogant boor, Mary beheld a quiet, independent man.

Tom was tall, lanky, and good-looking in spite of having shifty green eyes. She only saw greased-back hair, Elvis style, a hint of a smile that vanished in a flicker, and an insolence she should never have mistaken for anxiety. Though when Dan and Matt finally met him, their first impression was that of someone who'd been hauled in after spending a night in a back alley. It was Mary's inability to make waves that caused her to mistake this coward for a forlorn fixer-upper. She took pity on the fact that he stuttered at times, especially when angry, and had only a grade school education. To Mary, he was everything Al wasn't, and she soon found herself married for the second time.

Mary knew Tom was mamba-tempered, yet she overlooked these small imperfections. Being married to Tom came with a price, and Mary paid with her self-esteem, which took a daily emotional or physical beating. Even deferring to him didn't make a difference once they were married. Everything made him angry now. Crazy angry. He had all the faults with none of the benefits and exercised control with his fists. She worried the boys would be next, but she was stuck; she was dependent on Tom to help pay the bills and unsure how to slip out of the marriage without creating a disaster.

"I hate the old geezer," Dan complained to Matt, who remained hopeful that this new dad would teach him how to throw a baseball and maybe make Dan quit picking on him. Even after a rare shower, Tom emitted the stench of grease and distrust, so ultimately Dan was right; he clashed with Tom from the start.

While the boys readied themselves for school, Tom appeared from downstairs, already scruffy and disheveled.

"He looks like a dog shaking himself after falling into the Sangamon River," Dan said just loud enough for Tom to know he'd said something sarcastic. If things were bad with Al, they were worse with Tom

"WH-WH-WHERE THE H-H-HELL HAVE YOU B-B-BEEN?" Tom smashed his dirty plate into the sink, where it shattered to pieces, and stormed into the living room. His stuttering intensified when he was excited or angry.

"We had a busy dinner crowd, Tom. You know how it is." Mary tried to keep her voice steady and not let on that he scared the hell out of her. She motioned for Matt and Dan to go upstairs, which they did.

Dan pulled a baseball bat from the closet and paced across the floor. The shouting from below sickened Matt, and he held his stomach, rocking back and forth on the edge of the bed.

"What are you doing with that bat?" An uneasy feeling brought Matt to his feet, born from having been the victim of some of Dan's previous assaults and knowing he'd used a weapon before.

Dan glared unblinkingly, pausing now and then to bounce the edge of the bat off one hand or act like he was going to bash Matt over the head, then laughing when his younger brother put his hands up in defense.

"You think your hands can stop a bat, moron? A bat would break your hands. If someone ever comes after you with a bat you better run or move fast if you ain't got no weapon to fight back with."

"We should get a dog to protect us. Everyone else has one," Matt lamented, hoping Dan would agree with him on the obvious benefits of owning a snarling, lunging attack dog in this section of town clogged with petty street criminals and racial hatred. Theirs was a neighborhood of leaky ceilings, broken appliances, and barking dogs. Residents understood the need for a weapon, and often, a German shepherd was the weapon of choice. Every car that squealed down the road initiated a chorus of savage growls that spread down the street like a wave from one house to the next before ebbing and then starting up again when another car would pass.

The shouting downstairs continued, interrupted only by the occasional sound of the refrigerator door slamming, assumedly

10

followed by the fizzing *crack* of a beer can popping open, until Tom had consumed enough canned ale to imagine himself the hapless victim of Mary's by now mostly forgotten offense. In an instant, he ended the fight by picking up the coffee table Mary had purchased at a secondhand store and swinging it across her back, breaking it into pieces like a scene out of an old western movie. It was one of his favorite moves.

Later, Matt tossed and turned on his bed, twisting the blankets this way and that as though the perfect position could cover up the fear and pain that lingered long after the fight had quieted. What had begun with Mary's piercingly painful screams faded to gentle sobs and eventually two sets of feet on the stairs and the click of a bedroom door. Dan wasn't sleeping either, Matt knew because the room lacked the comforting breathing pattern of his brother's snoring that carried the weight of nearly full pubescence. Instead, the room pulsed with a cold silence that left Matt feeling alone.

From the quiet, a small rumpling sound rose from Dan's bed. Matt's head jerked in response. Perhaps, he dared to hope, Dan was sitting up and preparing to ask Matt what was wrong; why he wasn't asleep yet. This childlike innocence allowed him to imagine that Dan might gently insist that Matt confide his deepest fears and pour out all his hurts before basking in the comfort of an older brother's wisdom which would contain the solution to all their problems. He'd seen it happen in a movie.

Dan was on his feet now, shoving his arms into an expensive leather jacket he kept hidden from Mary and Tom. Matt felt his pillow pulled from beneath him and then slammed across his face.

"If you're coming with me you got two minutes," Dan hissed, giving the side of Matt's bed a quick kick.

Compared to home, which drained him of hope, the streets felt enchanted. The false promises of a better life tugged at the boys' desires. By 11 PM, they'd climbed out the window into the cool air and onto the porch overhang before shimmying down the pillar.

Matt felt a wisp of relief when he released his grip on the house and jumped free. He and Dan wouldn't wander too long on the streets at this hour. Likely Dan had a destination in mind as he usually did, a friend's house, the hidden corner of an empty lot where small groups of barely teenage boys gathered to do whatever boys of that age do this late on a school night. If Henry was buying, and he usually was, they'd search for good spots to heist anything of value on their way to wherever they were going. Tom and Mary would never know they'd left unless trouble erupted and they got hauled in by the police. And he could count the number of times that had happened in the last few months on two hands.

Chapter 3
Black and White

Springfield, Illinois, had a long history of racial tensions. This capital city seethed in bitterness between strict southern settlers and black inhabitants. Hostilities had flared on and off since the mid-1800s. In 1908 white residents rioted against black residents, resulting in two black men unjustifiably lynched, while four white men were killed by retaliating gunfire. Many of the antagonistic sentiments endured time and now haunted Matt and Dan on a regular basis.

When they'd first moved to Springfield, the boys attended school at Iles Elementary, a nearby public school, with no inkling that Mary would eventually enroll them in Catholic school. Matt planned to take a different route home from Iles, but ultimately it backfired. This morning Dan had promised to meet him at the front door of the school. Matt waited, pressed up against the building, for ten minutes and the yard was almost cleared out. He moved warily. Both boys felt defenseless among the racial tensions that flared up frequently in this predominantly black area of town. Their pale skin made the streets extra dangerous for two "honkies" or "crackers" as they were often called by anyone, even strangers, passing them on the streets. Bullies crossed the racial barriers, and the white trash bullies were just as vicious and dangerous. Then there were the leather jackets emblazed with bright colors that bragged *Ghetto Ghosts, Southside Savages, Kingsmen,* or *War Lords.* These gangs lurked in unexpected places and each controlled a different neighborhood where the members prowled, seeking out opportunities to intimidate those not affiliated with their ilk to join. Matt couldn't wait at the school much longer without the risk of being caught alone like last week when a group of sixth-grade boys had followed him, laughing and taking turns kicking him in the butt all the way to his front door. Tom asked what the hell had taken him so long to get home after school, to which Matt replied that going through this neighborhood was like trying to get across the Serengeti safely.

"The Sarah Getty? Who the hell is that?" Tom said, hands on hips, with that slack-mouthed perplexed look that never failed to irritate Matt.

So he folded his arms across his stomach, put his head down, and walked away from the school. He crossed the street to avoid a disheveled man hell-bent on yelling at a telephone pole and kept walking until he got to a safe-looking side street void of kids hanging out on the front steps. As far as he could see there were only slumping houses with paint that curled up from the boards like skin from a sunburn. Occasionally the cry of a baby or a snarling dog throwing itself against a screen door broke the silence. His radar went up whenever a broken muffler screeched on a nearby street or the howl of a siren wailed in the distance. Matt was learning to check every street to find the safest route. He mastered the art of looking straight ahead and not making eye contact, yet he couldn't help noticing the old man by the curb loudly banging the lid back onto the trash can and giving Matt one of those hateful stares that made it clear he was the wrong color to be in this neighborhood. Just when he thought of crossing to the other side of the street, kind of zigzagging like he read you were supposed to do if chased by an alligator, no other than Samuel, the biggest and oldest kid in the class, threw open the screen door of the house right next to Matt. Samuel had slits for eyes and a blossoming afro that made him appear even taller than he was. Matt had never seen him smile. Having been held back in both kindergarten and first grade, Samuel not only couldn't read but he was an angry fourth-grader who couldn't read. Matt kept walking, and Samuel pursued him with a rooster strut.

"Hey, honky, what you doin' at my house? Come to steal my shit?" Samuel laughed, more of a guttural cackle really, which caused Matt to walk faster though he refused to run in part due to Dan's oft-repeated words: *It's better to be dead than to be a coward.* Samuel locked step with Matt before falling directly behind him. At school, Samuel was famously loud, and Matt hoped this was one of those days he just wanted to bluster. Samuel's merciless eyes bored into Matt from behind; he could feel it. Without warning a rock bounced off the back of Matt's head followed by the same threatening laughter that knotted his stomach. If he could just make it a few more blocks . . .

WHAM! Matt's head snapped at the sound of something crashing against the side of a house. It only took a second for Matt to figure out he was being set up.

"Hey, Isaiah, get out here, this white honky jus' threw a rock at yo' house!" Samuel yelled toward the open window of a home that sagged with the shame of its cracked green paint and square of plywood nailed across the front window. Matt kept walking. Samuel grabbed onto his shirt, with flickering eyes that indicated he was encouraged by someone shouting a response from inside the house. Samuel dragged Matt toward the house to the thunder of a chair scraping across a floor and then the screech of the screen door being thrown open. Matt pulled away, but Samuel pummeled him from behind. Before Matt could react, a flurry of shoes kicked at his face as he scrambled to get back on two feet. Suddenly he felt the painful thud of an elbow to his mouth and the crunch of teeth. Blood trickled to the back of his throat and powerful hands knocked him to the ground. He glanced up to see Samuel's fist coming at him.

"Hold his arms! Hold his arms down, Isaiah!"

Samuel straddled atop him like a cowboy.

"I'm gonna redden his head," Samuel drawled, pounding away like a jackhammer against Matt's forehead with the curled up middle finger of his right hand while Matt squirmed beneath, cursing himself for not knowing he walked right past Samuel's house.

"Gimme a turn on that boy!" the unfamiliar kid named Isaiah said, shoving Samuel's hand away. Then he leaned in with one hand on Matt's chest and thumped his forehead with the other. "Tell me you're a baby, and I'll stop," he taunted with a gleam in his eyes. "Come on, whitey, say *I'm a baby!*"

Matt broke one arm free and lunged for a fistful of hair, but Isaiah was fast and moved out of the way laughing. A hot wetness built up beneath Matt's eyelids, and he suddenly resented his white skin. A sick hatred fueled his anger, and he powered himself to a sitting position just as a figure appeared on the porch, startling Matt, who was twisting to free his hands from Samuel's grip.

A sharp voice shouted at them from a distance, and the grip slackened. "WHAT *ARE* YOU DOIN' TO THAT BOY?"

Samuel's face fell, then froze when the hefty woman came storming their way. Her expression left Matt confused as to whether she was coming to help or perhaps just watch.

"You got that boy good, now get his white ass off this street! And I don't wanna see him round here no more makin' trouble neither." By now, she loomed over all of them like a storm cloud, pointing a finger at Matt and pulling the other boys up by their collars. Samuel grinned and hawked up a wad of snot that he aimed at Matt's face. Skilled at dodging Dan's loogies, Matt ducked and then turned to see a wad of slime running down his arm.

What he felt wasn't sadness but rather hatred. The last time anyone around here had shown him concern was when he was seven and rode his bike on the street right into the path of an oncoming car. The terrified lady who ran him over lifted him into her car and raced to the hospital with reassurances that "everything will be just fine." Matt pleaded with her not to tell his mom for fear

16

his bike would get taken away. He diligently pressed the wad of napkins she gave him to the bloody welt on his temple while floating in and out of consciousness. His mom found out, of course, but the bike was mangled beyond repair in what Mary called an act of God, and she praised the woman for having the good sense to bring him to a doctor instead of running off like people around here normally did.

A few days later, squinting to adjust to a moonless night, Dan and Matt crept out of the upper window and edged silently down the pillar. Just to test his prowess, Matt controlled his movements, creeping silently like a tarantula and careful not to catch a sliver on the splintered wood. They walked by Samuel's house, but there was a light on, and the two didn't even have to confer about what to do next but wisely walked on. Down the street and around the corner was an empty lot.

"Watch this!" Matt floated across the gravel soundlessly with the only response being Dan's unimpressed eye roll. "You act like it's no big deal because the ground crunches beneath your big fumble feet. I have a new nickname for you: Captain Crunch. Don't try to sneak around with Captain Crunch; he can't walk on cotton balls without making noise."

"Yeah? How quiet are you when you land on the ground?" Dan picked him up below the armpits and slammed him onto the gravel.

With the pecking order reestablished, they spent an hour on target practice under a flickering street lamp, seeing who was the most accurate at hitting a particular brick with a rock. On the way back home, all the lights were off in Samuel's house. At 1:30 AM, a large rock went crashing against Samuel's front window, sending a spider web of cracks across the dingy glass.

Chapter 4
Shakedown

The next morning they jerked awake to Mary yelling in the doorway of their bedroom. There was only a hint of sunshine peeking in the window at this early hour, but light from the hallway poured into the bedroom, and the familiar morning scents of fresh coffee and cigarette smoke spilled into the room. Dan pulled a pillow over his head. Matt wasn't sure whether to listen or tune her out, so he took a cue from Dan and turned over with heavy eyes hoping to fall back to sleep. He'd slept in an erratic haze filled with thoughts of dread and panic.

"The devil's got both of you now! You know that, don't you? I know you snuck out last night! Don't think you can fool me!" She rambled on as usual about going down the wrong road with Satan. Matt noticed her voice sounded huskier; perhaps from years of smoking and drinking coffee, he theorized. Dan shut the door on her, and they dressed—Matt pulled on the T-shirt and blue jeans he'd dropped on the floor before bed last night—but she continued the rant from behind the closed door and even followed them downstairs despite Dan making a poor attempt at looking as though he were brushing past her when he'd clearly thrown an elbow.

She hovered over them with one arm perched across her stomach, the elbow of the other arm resting atop it and a stream of smoke spewing from her nostrils. "You're going to end up in jail! You know that, don't you?"

Downstairs Dan catapulted a spoonful of mushy cereal at Matt, who then kicked back in retaliation beneath the table.

"It's Monday," Dan said to Mary and held out his hand.

She shook her head in defeat before handing them each a dollar with a terse reminder not to lose it, or they'd have no milk money for the rest of the week. Listening to her tirade was the price they were required to pay for her forgiveness. Their family lived in the moment, so once the storm blew over, the boys would go back to their old ways and sneak out again in a few nights. They all knew this was the pattern but were unequipped to change the dysfunction.

Matt ended that school day slouched in a wooden chair waiting to see the principal. Phones rang in the background, and the secretary threw him occasional looks of contempt as though his presence somehow interrupted her work. He already hated the principal—hated everyone at this school. He was dreading the thought of the principal imposing some unfair punishment on him. More than the punishment itself, he despised someone else being in control of his life because this meant that he wasn't. Experience taught him that being at the mercy of someone else's decisions was terrifying.

For some reason, he'd had a fierce case of an overactive bladder earlier today and had been unable to avoid going to the restroom. One of the many places he avoided. No sooner had he stepped into the restroom than two older boys appeared out of nowhere.

"I'll be the lookout," the heavier boy said, stationing himself at the doorway while Matt considered his limited options. There were two of them, both older than Matt, which ruled out fighting. That about covered his choices.

"Empty your pockets," the other boy said, slamming Matt against the wall. It was a shakedown, strong-arm robbery, and it could happen anywhere. He was forced to empty his pockets, and there was no use trying to fight when outnumbered. Matt tried to palm the dollar he'd carelessly left in his pocket due to poor planning from a lack of sleep last night. The boy grabbed Matt's hand, plucked the dollar, and was on his way with one last shove for good luck.

Since that moment, something hadn't sat right with him. Why was it that the things he worked so hard to learn outside of school were the opposite things he was expected to do inside of school? Just this morning he left home early, even though he'd hardly gotten any sleep, just so that he could walk partway to school with Dan for protection. All on his own he figured out that he needed to vary his route as well as what time he left the house for school, so no one knew exactly where to find him. Then he discovered a place behind a garage near the school with no barking dogs where he could wait until the bell rang for school to start. On the way to the playground, he spotted a young boy walking all alone who made the mistake of brandishing a brand new pencil in the air as if it were a sword. Matt shoved the boy with his elbow, harder than necessary, grabbed the pencil, and slipped it into his coat pocket. Of course, Samuel with his all-seeing eye saw this and in turn took the pencil from Matt's pocket while they were standing in line. Matt shoved him and took his pencil back. When Samuel howled as if he'd been knifed in the gut, the teacher automatically believed him. So now Matt sat here, with a slight smirk as his only armor and nodding as though he agreed, while the principal barked at him. No one ever said, *"Nice job, Matt! You survived a shakedown, found your own pencil instead of asking to borrow one, protected yourself from that bully Samuel, and got your own property back. I guess you know everything you need to know. You can go home for the rest of the day."*

School was torture for Matt. Aside from the rigidity of heavy wooden desks in neat rows and endless assignments scrawled in white across the chalkboard, the lessons moved too slowly. He could consume a book in the time his classmates had plotted through three chapters. On those rare days when he chose to do the work, he breezed through math problems like an accountant.

Bending to the teacher's instructions too often left him feeling powerless, so he frequently reassured himself that he was still in control of his life by bucking her authority on a regular basis. Much of the time, he preferred regressing into his own creative daydreams where he sketched pictures and made himself the champion of a drag-racing competition. Other times he'd create detailed buildings with angular shapes. He was bored, and the only thing he had to occupy his mind was how to avoid being bullied in the classroom, the bathroom, the hallway, and especially before and after school on the blocks surrounding Iles Elementary. The streets were more dangerous, and Matt couldn't even count the number of times he'd been shaken down or had to fight his way home.

"Take your shoes off, too, bitch!" they said.

"Yeah, white boy's prob'ly hidin' his money in his socks or somethin'."

Sometimes they took the entire contents of his lunch and ate it right on the spot. He avoided taking the same route home two days in a row but always bypassed the abandoned parking lots and litter-strewn alleys. Once home, he hoped Dan hadn't been bullied or he'd take it out on Matt. Tom usually wasn't there, but when he was, no one was safe. And today, Tom was coming home after work. Mary had warned the boys to have their chores done or else.

Chapter 5
Bruises that Last a Lifetime

"Did you wash the dishes? It's your turn." Matt stuck his head out of the bathroom where he was attempting to clean a scratched tub, stained and permanently brown, and yelled upstairs to Dan. Matt couldn't reach the sink without standing on a chair, and the last time he'd stood on a chair it tipped and broke a handle off Tom's favorite mug, and Dan took a hammer after Matt before spending the better part of an hour trying to glue the handle on and threatening Matt that he owed him for this favor.

"Nah, I'll get to them later." Dan combed his hair hard in an attempt to make it look longer, but the short strands just bounced back up. He'd skipped school with his friends and the notion that he could do whatever he wanted carried over into the brothers' conversation.

Matt paused, hoping to weave together just the right words to make Dan realize he'd be better off doing the dishes rather than whatever it was he was doing in his bedroom before Tom stormed into the house. As a bonus, he could use it as proof that he was responsible enough to take care of a dog, something he'd been trying to convince Mary of for months now. He brought up the topic every time he could segue it into the conversation, and two nights ago he made the valid point that "We are literally the only family on this block without a dog," to which Mary opened her

23

mouth to reply but ended up wordlessly tugging at the broken zipper of her vinyl purse to extract another cigarette before flipping on the television and staring at it for the rest of the night.

He flicked off the whirring vacuum, thankful that the temperamental beast hadn't given out. "The carpet's clean!" He waited for a response from Dan, who was grunting out his umpteenth set of push-ups on the bare floor, but none came. "Good thing, too. Tom'll be home soon." Matt tried to add the last part very nonchalantly and took a second glance into the bathroom before rubbing a smear off the wall with his shirt. He wanted to give a final inspection to the bedroom he shared with Dan before heading downstairs to do the dishes his brother was avoiding.

Dan, in a worn undershirt, flexed in front of the full-length mirror which hung crookedly on the back of the bedroom door. "Tom doesn't scare me, you little worm." He deepened his voice to sound older and then curled one side of his mouth down and narrowed his eyes. Matt moved to the other side of the room and glanced out of habit at the saucer-sized hole in the ceiling that sometimes dropped bits of plaster on their heads. He sat on the edge of one of the sagging twin beds, watching Dan, and tried out a few scowling grimaces of his own. Dan was taller and older by three years. He'd made new friends recently who were older and hung out on a deserted street corner across from the pool hall, making crude jokes and spewing insults to each other at lightning speed. Cracking, it was called, and the fastest, wittiest cracker earned the highest respect. They entertained themselves by intimidating kids who walked by or by pitching pennies when they were supposed to be in school. Heck, some of them, like Henry, weren't even in school anymore, having dropped out to pursue opportunities on the street. At only fifteen years old, Henry looked all of twenty, had served time in the state's juvenile training school, and now ran a thriving business fencing stolen goods.

"Don't stare at his scar like a f****** loser!" Dan warned, referring to the purplish mark that ran from Henry's left eye almost down to his mouth, a reminder that he had and would fight at any hint of a threat. Reluctantly, Dan gave in to Matt's pleas a few weeks ago and brought him along to meet this new friend. The first glimpse Matt caught of Henry was that of a large frame sitting atop a small stool beneath the sagging overhang of a porch where he was tossing grapes into the air and catching them in his open mouth, looking like a bullfrog snatching flies out of the air. Henry's mountainous afro made him appear even more massive, and he had a solidness to him, like a ghetto statue swaddled in a leather flight jacket. He never deviated from his trademark scowl. Matt didn't let Dan see the way he cowered when Henry met his eyes with that cold stare. But, for the right price, such as a heisted car, Henry was willing to overlook Dan's pale skin and even looked after Matt providing business was good. For Henry and Dan, it was the dysfunctional marriage of power and desperation, with Matt the third wheel, following in Dan's good fortune as always.

The two brothers had few options though. The fortunate kids had older siblings or cousins skilled in the art of street survival. The unlucky ones, those new to the neighborhood, for example, were plucked up by street gangs and crime rings who smooth-talked the new recruits into doing a small favor in exchange for a valuable service such as protection from a dangerous bully. The thankful newcomer would quickly find himself under the control of this supposed savior and would soon be required to perform large favors for a small return. Without this protection, though, he would have to scamper through the neighborhood no safer than a hunted rabbit, dashing behind this house and slipping through that alley knowing that the days were numbered before disaster struck.

Dan, with his unruly brown hair and an uncanny knack for slipping through loopholes, found a niche somewhere in between all of this. For the right price, Henry, who had a circle of powerful cohorts yet wasn't part of a gang, was willing to look after Dan and Matt providing they delivered what he wanted.

"Matt, I tell you to go do certain things for me and you do it, then you come let me know if someone be messin' wich ya," Henry explained through narrowed eyes while rubbing out a cigarette with the tip of his steel-toed shoes. His voice sounded as though it had been buffed with sandpaper.

These friends gave Dan more confidence on the street but not here at home. His self-esteem, though unfortunately not his muscles, bulged in the presence of these friends. Not one of them would think of backing down from a fight no matter how formidable the opponent might be. Dan didn't hesitate to pound Matt over brotherly differences, but there was no way he could handle Tom on his own. Matt bit his lip and imagined what his life would be like when Tom finally went overboard and really hurt Dan someday.

The front door creaked open below them followed by a slam. An inside door slammed followed by a loud flush that echoed through the thin walls of the entire house. Matt sat still chewing his fingernails and watched as Dan turned slowly from the mirror, pulled on a faded sweatshirt, and absentmindedly shoved his pair of good shoes further and further under the bed.

"Did you do the dishes?" he asked Matt in such a quiet voice that it came out as a squeak.

On the floor below someone was walking from room to room. There was the muffled swearing of a man's voice and the slamming of a cupboard which sifted upward. It was clear from the start that to Tom they were just Mary's kids and second best if that, and he used any excuse to berate or belittle them. More than once, the cutting pain of Tom's cruelty had torn through Matt. A stair step creaked. Pause. Another creak. Another pause. They knew Tom moved slothily on purpose just to draw out the suspense and make them anxious. Matt realized he had to pee, but the only bathroom was downstairs. The bedroom door didn't have a lock, and the handle was so loose it could probably be pulled off with a few hard yanks so there was no chance of locking Tom out. Not that it would do any good. They'd have to come out sometime. He turned to Dan, who stood rigidly near the painted green dresser they shared, whose nervous breaths rattled out like a squeak through his nose. Matt hoped the reason Dan was standing there with his mouth pursed tightly and shaking was because he was gearing up to protect them from Tom. After several tense and eternally long minutes, the handle turned, and the door opened a few inches. There was a long pause. Then Tom kicked the door so hard it banged against the wall, rattling everything in the room.

"Downstairs," he shrieked and slammed the door against the wall one more time for effect. The door vibrated on its hinges, and Matt's insides turned acidy.

Downstairs the boys sat rigidly on the couch. Matt nervously rubbed at one of the smaller cigarette burns that dotted the plaid cushions. The room was sparsely furnished yet cluttered, which was a challenge to Tom, who tended to bumble rather than walk.

"If there's a space to be had, you got some damn piece of crap sittin' on it!" he'd yelled at Mary one time after knocking over a vase and breaking it.

It was one of the only things Tom had ever said that caused Matt to agree. Lately, she'd taken to collecting angels as if their presence could somehow obliterate the hatred that simmered in the house. Over by the one wooden chair and end table, carefully arranged by Mary with knickknacks to cover every scratch, Tom shed his belt with relish. He strutted past a black-and-white TV propped atop a table with foil-covered rabbit ear antennas that only seemed to work if the weather was good, and struck what Matt considered to be an embarrassing attempt at a James Dean scowl. Tom stood before them, swatting the folded belt against one palm, pausing, and watching with exhilaration for signs of fear. When neither Matt nor Dan pleaded or cowered, Tom swore under his breath, lurched back a step, and clenched his teeth, before unleashing the leather end of the belt on Dan and then Matt's bare skin, alternating the hot lashes between the two and working up a stain of perspiration on the underarms of his T-shirt. Once Tom passed a certain point it was as if a switch flipped and his anger exploded into uncontrollable rage. Both boys sickened when they saw it happen.

27

"Y-y-y-you b-b-better, y-y-you, y-y-you better l-listen when I tell you t-t-t-o, t-t—, t-to have those damn dishes washed when I get home!" He flailed the belt against their bare skin over and over, working himself into a froth until he finally collapsed, exhausted and wheezing, onto a chair.

***

They didn't go back to school for the rest of the week until the welts and bruises that couldn't be covered by long sleeves lightened to pale pinks. Tom and Mary argued about that too, because Mary did not want them to miss school. The bruises were the visible reminders; it was the unseen scars on his psyche that had most affected Matt. His ability to understand the injustice of Tom's attacks combined with Matt's inability to voice his frustrations created a toxic situation that was at least partially responsible for turning him from a hopeful child into an ill-tempered misanthrope.

"You're setting a precedent. Pretty soon they'll start getting the idea on their own to skip for any reason that seems good enough. Believe me, I know," Mary insisted. But in the end, Tom won. So there was nothing to do all day but help Henry with odd jobs. With no need to get up early for school the next day, they resorted to sneaking out of the bedroom window every night to roam through the neighborhood under the cover of dark with no clear intent other than to cause a little noise and irritation.

"For a couple white boys you lookin' whipped," Henry said when they arrived the next evening with a sack of stolen goods. "You get in a fight at school?"

Neither of them answered.

Henry cast his eyes down and wisely let it drop.

Working as a team, Matt and Dan had stolen a bottle of Imperial whiskey, some cologne, and a pair of sneakers for Henry. The sneakers were the hardest, but Matt distracted the clerk while Dan took the shoes from the box and stuck them in the waistband of his pants. Dan was a good shoplifter, but soon the student would surpass the teacher.

By now, Matt didn't have much trouble with "the brothers" on the street. He had Henry, whose dark skin no longer mattered since Matt had grown to like him. Everyone knew the pecking order, and everyone knew that Matt and Dan fell under the jurisdiction of Henry. The hate and the hard stares continued, but people kept to themselves, and Matt convinced himself this was tolerable. What he worried about was honing his criminal prowess so he didn't get caught. Most of the jobs Henry assigned him involved stealing from one of the small drugstores or hardware stores, and some of the employees were suspicious of him already. With a deep-seated urge to deceive and prevail, this was just the incentive he needed to perfect his flair for shoplifting.

Chapter 6
Switchblades and Stilettos

It was nearly dusk when Matt decided to head to the drugstore five blocks away. Mary and Tom were working late, or the house would have been filled with the aroma of pork chops or meatloaf instead of the stale cigarette smoke that lingered pervasively. It would have been wiser to leave an hour ago, but he'd just found another nickel under Tom and Mary's bed. He knew all the places to check where a coin might have fallen out of Tom's pockets while he was in a drunken stupor—between the couch cushions, under the bed, anywhere in the bedroom really. Now Matt had enough money to buy some Bazooka bubblegum and maybe candy cigarettes which would give him a reason to be in the store, and he could heist more expensive items for Henry at the same time. Using his shoulder, he leaned against the cabinet in the living room with all his strength to push it away from in front of the door and back to where it belonged. He put it there so no one could break the door down while he was home alone.

Once he left the safety of home, he exposed himself to a different set of dangers. The porches of most houses were by now bristling with men sitting splay-legged with their cans of beer and smoking cigarettes while the women stood at the edges, trading snippets of news with each other and watching the younger kids who were toddling up and down the front steps or chasing dogs. Matt ignored the mocking taunts shouted to him as he passed several of these tired homes even though hatred toward these strangers who hurled abuse at him simmered through to the surface of his skin.

"Hating just hardens your own heart," Mary preached to him, but Matt thought she should have been telling that to the neighbors.

He had nearly reached the store when just ahead, two men burst through the doorway of a bar, shoving each other until they both ended up in the middle of the street. Matt backtracked a few steps, but then, emboldened by the growing crowd and curious, he ran up ahead to get a good look.

"YOU MOTHERF***ER! I'll cut yo' heart out!" one of the men, a burly guy in his early twenties, shouted while pulling a knife out of his pocket and swinging it wildly at the other man. Meanwhile, a crowd swelled seemingly out of nowhere, like flies to a piece of fresh dung, emerging from windowless bars and dank alleyways, and egging them on. A glint of light reflected off the silver blade as the weapon slashed through the air. Matt had seen a few of these fights in the last year since many people carried stilettos or switchblades. He stood watching, feeling both excited and frightened. The insults flew and the second man, smaller but very fast, ran at the burly man clutching his own white-handled switchblade. His swift jabs landed first in the bicep then the upper chest until blood gushed down in huge splotches onto the man's tattered shirt.

"It's over, man! Let it be done!" someone yelled from the crowd, presumably one of the stabbed man's friends, who then broke up the fight.

"Yeah, well he best not be messin' with my s**t no more," the victor yelled to no one in particular, wielding his bloody knife and showing it to the crowd as he strutted away.

Someone pushed their way to a pay phone, and soon the wail of an ambulance grew louder while Matt considered that the same thing could happen to him someday, but he concentrated on the lights twirling in the reflection of the store window. It was a nice distraction while he shoplifted his way through the store. Before slipping a flashlight in his pocket, he checked the "peep hole." To curb shoplifting, the elderly pharmacist had drilled a small hole, just big enough for his eye, in the wall between the store and the room where he filled prescriptions, enabling him to look out among the customers. If the eye was watching, Matt browsed; if the eye was absent, he proceeded to steal. The old man caught a lot of people, but he never caught Matt.

The clerk eyed him uncertainly, but then some commotion around the ambulance caught her attention, and she walked wide-eyed to the window. While Matt continued filling his pockets, the bloodied man was loaded onto a stretcher and carted off. The next day Matt saw the same guy standing across the street from the school with his chest and arm wrapped in white gauze. He had his head bent down and was handing something in his curled up fist to one of the kids lined up waiting to buy something from him.

Chapter 7
Spike

On the street, brains were good. Brawn was better. If you had neither, you plummeted to the bottom and became fodder for anyone who could out-fool or out-power you. If you had both, along with the ability to command respect, you rose straight to the top of the dung heap. The most inferior specimens had to work twice as hard to earn the good graces of the alpha male, and the alpha had to work twice as hard as those in the middle to maintain his position. Those in the middle either had to work to break into the upper ranks before a misstep sent them in the opposite direction. No one got to skate.

A few months after meeting Henry, Dan won the bodyguard lottery when he befriended one of the few white guys in the neighborhood. At fifteen, Spike, whose real name was Bill, wore his dark hair long and untrimmed. He was six feet tall, 200 pounds of mean street fighter, and earned his nickname because he carried a railroad spike in his rear pocket at all times which he used in three ways: he would stab with the pointed end, club with the blunt end, or hold the spike in his closed fist to give solid weight to his punch. Spike didn't hesitate to use the weapon, which clinched his reputation as a loose cannon. Dan and Spike made extra money at night rolling drunks or beating up a lone walker and then stealing his wallet. Every week Spike made a new plan for one of these strong-arm robberies and tracked the hits on a map so they weren't too predictable.

This grimy, hard-faced street rat had even less family than Matt and Dan. He'd been removed from the custody of his dad, who spent his days and nights strung out on heroin and was too sick and broken down to work. The two of them had lived in one room of a former motel that was converted into a flop house. There'd been one bed, dirty and without so much as a sheet to cover it, and cockroaches that climbed the walls even during broad daylight. Spike now lived with his aging grandparents and immediately gravitated toward Dan's family and even tried to take Matt under his wing.

"If I had a mom who cared about me that much I'd never let her get treated that way," he said upon first learning of Tom's violent nature.

Spike showed up in their kitchen at dark, as he often did, and grabbed Matt from behind in a chokehold, responding with a gentle chuckle when the boy gagged and turned red before working himself free with a twist and a pull. Spike smiled in approval.

"You're gettin' stronger." His hand glided curiously over one of Mary's angels, stern-faced but with a chip in each wing, which guarded the table.

Tom was rumbling in the next room, but they both ignored it until a blood-freezing scream sent them both running to the living room door where they found Tom shoving Mary against the wall, *you spend too much damn money on them damn thankless kids*, and cocking back his fist. Dan had been in the process of coming into the kitchen but now stood wide-eyed and trapped like a rabbit between Tom and the doorway. Matt felt Spike go rigid before he locked eyes on Tom and strutted over to give him a warning shove.

"You hit her again, and you'll hit the floor." He stepped closer to Tom and kept his eyes leveled. The room stilled.

Tom was the worst type of coward, only able to intimidate women and children, and unaccustomed to facing someone stronger than himself.

Tom forced a nervous chuckle. "Oh yeah, kid? H-h-how about y-y-you get the hell out of my house?"

Spike's eyes narrowed, and he lunged forward. That's when Matt saw the hunk of metal clutched in his fist. The spike came to life in an overhand motion, and the blunt end smashed into Tom's forehead with a sickening thud. Matt jumped back and held his breath, hoping Tom wouldn't beat them all. Dan didn't flinch. His eyes lit up, and a smile curled at the corners of his lips. Tom staggered backward on rubber legs, moaning and clutching his head until he collapsed into a worthless heap on the kitchen floor. Matt stood in awe of the way Spike towered motionlessly over Tom. Spike's hands didn't shake, and his mouth didn't quiver. Not even a little.

"That piece of crap better not beat you when I'm around." His eyes settled on Mary while he replaced the spike in his rear pocket and hiked his shirt back over it. Mary stood there stunned and silent. Spike nudged Matt, who was now feeling a smattering of hope that things would be better. The beatings continued for Mary but never when Spike was around.

The boys headed out into the night, shadowy figures, three abreast, but their paths would soon part. When someone barely more than a child has endured a lifetime of hate, neglect, and pain, the unbalance leaves its mark in the form of a hard-set mouth, cold eyes, and malfunctions within the neural pathways. Spike graduated from petty crimes to a host of violent felonies including armed robbery with a handgun. He went on to spend his entire adult life in a maximum security federal prison.

Chapter 8
Persistence

Mary huddled on the worn carpeting in the living room that was dim and gloomy even in daylight thanks to the yellowed drapes she kept pulled shut. She was choking back sobs. *Thank God, he doesn't know what else happened today.* Tom was on the couch, stuttering and blaming Mary that her boys had brought home a reeking street urchin who'd sucker punched him before he'd had a chance to kick the kid's butt. She knew Tom was partially right. Her heart broke every time the boys skipped school and calls from the police department were becoming regular. Dan had been in another fight or Matt had stolen from a store. She'd tried grounding them, but they took off every time she left the house, which was often.

"All this law-breaking will catch up with you! I swear it will. You'll be wishing you'd listened when you end up behind bars some night!" She yelled it to their backs until the door swung shut on her words, and the brothers disappeared into the dark.

Mary threw her arms in the air in response to Tom's blameful glare. "I'm not a warden. I can't lock them up here and stand guard all night. What am I supposed to do?" She badgered Tom, who just shook his head in disgust and slammed the door extra hard behind him before heading out into the night. Part of Mary wanted Tom here for company, yet she reveled in the thought of a peaceful evening. She shrugged and curled up on the couch with a beer and a romance novel. She and another waitress had traded books that day, and Mary confided to this friend how worried she was about the boys running with the devil and how she thought some good strict nuns could put them on the right road. Her boys were so smart. Not just street-wise but smart. As far as Mary could tell, Matt had taught himself to read. At the age of five, he'd memorized a book of nursery rhymes within days. Dan was sharp with facts and numbers, and with the right schooling, they could work their way right out of this butt crack section of the city. They just needed guidance, and she needed to find someone who could manage that job. Mary didn't admit even to her friend that half the time when she got home, the boys were nowhere to be found.

What they needed was to get into a good Catholic school, but there was no money for that. The kids at their current school were just out to get them. Matt was in another fight, and of course, the other kids said Matt started it. If Tom found out, there was no telling what he'd do. As the only white boy in his class, Matt was always to blame for the fights, but she had no luck convincing the principal of this.

"He's a good boy inside," she said, cutting off the principal before he could respond. "Him and Dan have been going to church every Sunday, and God's hand is ready to fill them both with the Holy Spirit. I have a strong feeling about it."

Mary dropped her boys off at the side door of the church every Sunday morning whether she felt like getting up or not. What she didn't know was that they never went inside. The two boys had discovered that a stack of papers got deposited on the front steps of the church, so they walked around to the main doors, heaved the bundle into Dan's arms, and walked to Sandy's Restaurant, where they stood outside the doors quickly hawking the entire load. Then they went inside and found a booth.

"God is good," Dan said, biting into his burger.

"It's like we found a reverse offering plate," Matt agreed.

"What the hell are you doing in there?" The voice sent Mary reeling upright from her hunched over position on the floor of the

40

bedroom closet where she was stuffing another six dollars into the jar she kept hidden from Tom and which now had a grand total of twenty-three dollars tucked away toward the boys' private school tuition. Seems she'd put a few bucks in and then have to take a few back out for one emergency or another. She hadn't heard Tom behind her because he'd crept into the house and tiptoed upstairs. Sneaking around was the only way he could keep tabs on his woman despite never having caught her anywhere she wasn't supposed to be. Yet.

"If you want to know what the hell I'm doing, don't sneak up on me!" she shouted, backing out of the closet and standing to face him. "Come right out and ask me. Like. A. Man." She paused slightly between each of the last three words. Mary knew it would cause a fight, but she wasn't going to make up a lie about what she'd been doing. She was not a liar. That was principle. So she started an argument and held her breath, hoping that he wouldn't get physical.

Tom's face turned ugly. He grabbed her by the hair and yanked her to the floor with Mary cursing at him the whole way down.

Tom was thin but strong. "Y-Y-YOU'RE YOU'RE YOU'RE A W-W-WASHED-UP, S-S-SMALL-TOWN B**CH!"

"You're a worthless husband! I work double shifts to support us while you drink up our money every night!"

"M-M-MAKE YOUR D-D-DAMN KIDS EARN THEIR OWN MONEY. I'M N-N-N-OT GONNA SUPPORT THEIR ROTTEN A**ES!"

"HELL, TOM! THEY'RE JUST KIDS! THEY CAN'T EVEN GET JOBS!"

Tom kicked her in the side of the head, not having a response to her logic, and grabbed a shoe to hit her with when a loud knock rattled the door downstairs. Tom was so close now she could smell the combination of sweat and fried food on his dirty work shirt.

"It's probably Spike," she whispered, not willing to unwrap her arms from around her head quite yet.

When Tom heard the name Spike, his bravado deflated like a balloon losing air, and he collapsed onto the bed. His voice quivered, then squeaked, "Get up and answer it!"

It was the newspaper boy at the door collecting for the month. Mary was waiting for him to show so she could cancel the paper. Although drinking coffee and reading the newspaper was her favorite way to start the day, this would be that much extra cash to put toward the boys' education. Mary knew how to make the best out of whatever she had.

"Hello, ma'am. This is my last week with the paper. I got a new job, so it'll be someone else next month." The boy was tall, thin, and black as the new bruise on Mary's arm, but he was always polite and on time. She supposed he had to be in order to earn tips around this place—and then the answer to her prayers just washed over her. Mary smiled wider than she had in months, paid the boy, and immediately made a phone call to the newspaper office.

Chapter 9
An Honest Living

Predawn, when crickets chirped the black sky into a shimmer of color, was Matt's favorite time of day. It was almost a safe kind of quiet, and he'd developed a sense for sizing up his vulnerability in different situations such as this one that felt too quiet for trouble. He sat with Dan on someone's front steps near the designated pick-up spot, making sure to avoid the tottering stack of garbage bags festering in a puddle of grayish muck. Matt plucked a few weeds from between the sidewalk cracks which he then carefully placed on Dan's hair just to see if he could without Dan noticing. Soon, a white van rumbled down the street, veered over to the curb, and a bundle of papers came flying out the door. Matt carried the cloth bag that hung to his knees, and Dan tossed the papers. They sauntered along, eyes scanning left and right just in case.

By the time the soft pink sky started to blue up, the streets began to yawn forth a straggle of early risers, and another paper was tossed onto their neighbor's porch. The paper route was routine, save for an occasional bully, and the two were always on the watch for several mean dogs along the way. As they approached the last house on the block, a rickety gray ramshackle of a place, they looked closely for Roscoe, a nasty half-Doberman, half-Labrador with an appetite for paperboys. The coast seemed clear, so Dan approached the house while Matt waited on the sidewalk. Suddenly there was a low growl followed by the shadow of a head popping up from behind the front steps. Dan froze in place, then immediately sprinted toward Matt, who'd already leaped onto the hood of a parked car. Roscoe raced toward the two, snapping at their threadbare heels, before clamping onto Dan's calf just as he scrambled onto the vehicle. Dan screamed and kicked, finally shaking Roscoe loose, and the two boys huddled together on the roof of the car while the dog circled them growling, pouncing, and barking. After several tense minutes, the front door of the house swung open and out walked a long-haired man wearing nothing but boxer shorts and appearing to have just crawled out of bed. He scolded the dog and gave his snout a quick slap before leading him into the house by the collar. "Come down off that car. I'll put this bad boy inside." With Roscoe safely gone, the boys continued down the street with Dan limping and sporting torn blue jeans and a set of puncture wounds in his calf from Roscoe's early morning greeting.

At home, he washed it off, covered it with cellophane tape since there were no bandages, and headed to school. No matter how much it hurt, the paper had to be delivered twice a day, morning and after school, or else people would call the newspaper office and complain. The office manager would call Dan's house, Tom would inevitably answer, and no dog bite could compare to the pain Tom could dish out.

Every night, the streets coughed up another batch of filth, so while delivering papers, Matt held his nose when walking past some of the dilapidated houses and buildings to ward off the stench of human waste that lingered in the seedier alleyways. Winos and strung-out druggies relieved themselves in these vacant spaces and then used old newspaper for toilet tissue. The scent of sick and sin lingered in the steamy air.

Each morning the boys delivered a paper to Rosalee, the shrewd house madam. Rosalee had a bejeweled appearance, typically wearing brightly colored blouses off the shoulder that revealed even more of her abundant chest than two paperboys should ever see. Bits of gold glittered and sparkled in her thick afro. Deep blue eyeshadow set off her skin, thick and the color of rum-soaked

Georgia clay. Deadly catlike fingernails fit her fiery temper, a necessary quality considering the rough clientele that often required more than a woman's touch. When she walked, her hips swung with enthusiasm, and she could flash a seductive smile one minute then go after an abusive john with hostility the next. She acted not only as a madam but as an accountant and house security as well. While other people carried knives, Rosalee was said to pack a .32 snub nose.

Matt and Dan actually looked forward to collection day since she paid on time, included a tip, they didn't have a dog to contend with, and they got a free peep at her girls. Rosalee lived in a two-story house with fading paint and windows clouded with cataracts of grime and smoke. The home's most distinctive feature, though, was a single light bulb painted bright red with fingernail polish that glowed day and night near the front door. The neighborhood whorehouse had anywhere from three to six girls turning tricks in any one of the four bedrooms.

"You wait right here on the porch while I get ya yore money," she said in a voice that was both breathy and tinted with a touch of brazen. With the door hanging wide open, the boys moved in as close as they dared to get their monthly glance into the parlor of Rosalee's house. The parlor was actually the living room where men would choose the girls who suited their fancy. On collection day, these girls were often sitting, scantily clad in long fishnet stockings and short skirts, on one of the three sofas in the parlor.

"Save up your money and come back in a few years," a girl in a low-cut blouse called out to both boys while adjusting the hem that exposed too much cleavage. The other girls laughed along with her, and Dan quickly moved the collection bag to cover his crotch.

As soon as Rosalee handed them the cash, they scrambled away red-faced yet already eager for next month's return. Matt's delight turned to suspicion when he caught a glimpse of a teenage boy across the street standing on the porch for what appeared to be no good reason.

"Hey, leave a couple dollars in the collection bag and hide the rest in case someone jumps us again," Matt suggested. His sixth sense kicked in.

"Nah, I'll just stick the bag under my shirt. No one will know I even have it."

They made it home without being harassed, but as the bag of money grew so did Matt's concern.

"Maybe Mom would give us the money," Matt suggested to Dan days later as they sat on the steps of their porch, not wanting to go inside. Dan replied with his half snort, half hopeless chuckle. They were finishing up collecting for the month when four boys with hoods pulled tight around their faces stole the money bag. Again.

They'd delivered papers all month for nothing. When they got home, they cornered Mary and refused to continue the paper route. Mary protested but then gave in rather than letting Tom overhear the argument.

"Well, at least I hope you learned a lesson from working an honest job," she said with satisfaction and held up one hand to indicate the conversation was over. They had. Honest, hard work didn't pay. Crime did.

Chapter 10
Man's Best Friend

Mary meant well. Even after years of living amongst people who took advantage of others, she refused to stop believing in the essential goodness of humanity, but that conviction didn't seem to get her anywhere in these parts. One of her customers was the proprietor from a local watering hole, the South Town Lounge. He locked his exceptionally ferocious white German shepherd, Chief, in the bar after hours to protect the premises. The dog flew into a demonic rage around everyone except his beloved owner, Bubba. After decades of eking out a living running a ragtag bar in a seedy neighborhood, Bubba decided to retire while he still had his liver. The problem was that he was moving to an apartment in a small town and wouldn't be able to take Chief with him. Usually, there were half a dozen regulars who were either looking for or knew someone who wanted a guard dog. Chief's unusually bloodthirsty nature was well-known throughout the area, so the customers jokingly refused offers to take the salivating dog home.

Matt lucked out that afternoon and found Dan hanging around after school, so the walk home seemed safer until they reached the sidewalk up to their own door. An explosive burst of angry snarling from just around the corner of the house sent the boys racing inside. "I think a mean dog is loose in our backyard!" the boys yelled to Mary, who seemed unaffected by the whole incident.

"He's not loose; he's on a chain," she answered without taking her eyes off the soap opera that was blaring and tapping her cigarette over an ashtray before taking a long sip of coffee.

The boys looked from one to another as if one of them might have an explanation.

A commercial for Palmolive came on, and Mary turned to the boys. Her face lit up in an unusual display of cheer. "You wanted a dog. I got you a dog," she said proudly, then motioned for them to follow her as she disappeared into the kitchen and pulled aside the curtain to the back door. There was Chief, wild-eyed and pinballing about the yard. Just then a man happened to come strolling down the back alley, and the beast started whipping around on his chain like a demonic flamenco dancer until he choked himself to the point that his barks were reduced to a squeak.

"You boys need to learn some responsibility. You wanna keep that dog, you're gonna have to take care of him," Mary admonished them.

Matt's mouth opened slightly, and he looked back and forth from Mary to the possessed beast contorting in the backyard, wondering if this was a joke. Dan crossed his arms over his stomach and chewed on the inside of his cheek, something he did when deep in thought.

"Bubba dropped him off this morning, and he seemed fine then, but . . . One of you needs to feed him and get him water. He ain't had anything to eat or drink all day cause he won't let me get near him now. That dog is vicious!"

"Matt's gonna feed that monster. He's the one who wanted a dog!" Dan made the first move before Matt could develop a strategy. After some futile arguing, Dan half shoved Matt out the door, where the younger boy clung to the edge of the house, straining to stay out of snapping distance of Chief. Mary slapped a peanut butter sandwich together and went back to her show while Dan taunted Matt through the open window.

"You won't have to feed him because that dog's gonna eat you for dinner!" Dan cracked the door open and shouted from behind his vantage point of safety before falling into fits of laughter.

Chief's leash allowed him to reach within four feet of the house, so with his back rubbing along the siding, Matt sidestepped over to a bag of dog food and a bowl at the corner of the house. He hoped that after a few minutes of barking, Chief would eventually see Matt wasn't a threat and would settle down. That didn't happen. Chief's ferocious snarls escalated, and Matt couldn't pull his eyes from the stake in the ground that was bending with every lunge. He dumped a pile of food into the bowl, talking to Chief in a soothing voice.

"You're a good dog, aren't you? Look what I have, Chief. Are you hungry? Don't bite the hand that feeds you—" Matt reached toward Chief with the bowl but quickly withdrew, sending chunks of food flying when the dog's vicious teeth came snapping within inches of his hand. He wondered if Dan might come out to help and glanced over at the window only to see his brother doubled over with laughter. "Come on, boy. Sit down so you can eat—" He set the bowl on the ground and slowly pushed it with his foot toward Chief, who once again came running and barking at full force. Matt jumped back, leaving the bowl in no-man's-land where it wasn't close enough for Chief to reach but also too far out of Matt's reach to grab it again. He finally got the idea to look in the alley and returned a few minutes later carrying a broken rake which he used to push the bowl over to Chief before retreating inside.

After a few days, Chief still hadn't warmed to Matt. Or anyone. His long-winded frenzies started up every time someone walked or drove down the street to the dismay of the neighborhood. Matt complained tirelessly about having to care for this wild beast. "That stake's gonna come loose, and he'll tear me apart one of these days!" he warned Mary. The next day, Matt returned to find the backyard empty. Mary had called Bubba and told him to come and get Chief.

Chapter 11
Nun of This Makes Sense

"We're the only dogless house in this city," Matt bemoaned, wadding up some homework and tossing it from the edge of the curb where he sat and into the gutter.

Dan pitched some loose rocks into the street and sneered. "Yeah, because you were too much of a baby to take care of the dog we had. We'll have to get you one of those girly dogs. A little poodle or something you can push around in a stroller."

Dan purposely lobbed his banana peel so it bounced off Matt's head before landing on his shoulder during a quick after-school bout of "cracking." Cracking was a necessary survival skill in this neighborhood. Whereas kids in a more affluent area might improve their standing through accomplishments on a Little League baseball team or brag about their dad's promotion at the bank, kids around here gained respect based on their ability to not only cleverly point out someone else's flaws or weaknesses but to be ready with a quick comeback when verbally attacked.

"You don't need no dog as long as you got that muttly girl to keep you company," Matt replied, referring to a girl Dan had been sneaking out of the house to meet. Cracking came naturally to Matt. He was one of the best in his class and had had unfettered opportunity for practice during a failed three-month stint at St. Patrick Catholic School, where he'd secured both the awe and fear of his classmates, whom he referred to as namby-pamby boys. Undeterred by the lack of cash, Mary had called around until she'd

51

found a Catholic school willing to take the boys based on financial hardship.

"No one gets anywhere in life without discipline. You've got to learn it!" she scolded both Dan and Matt after receiving a fourth discipline call from the school in four days. The principal added what a shame it was that a boy as brilliant as Matt was too insubordinate to amount to anything, but Mary didn't mention that, thinking Matt might consider this supposed intelligence a substitute for obedience.

"Them nuns are mean. They hate kids," Matt said, though he realized that he used his position as one of the biggest nine-year-olds in the school, along with his street smarts and quick temper, to intimidate the other kids. The nuns were on to him.

One looked directly at him yesterday while reading from the Bible: "'But the wicked are like the tossing sea, and the waters toss up mire and dirt.' Isaiah 57:20. Open your Bibles and turn to the passage now . . ."

Later, while the other kids were out enjoying recess, she harangued him with accusations of being self-centered, corrupt, and unholy. "No one can see how capable you are because you hide it beneath a blanket of sin!"

Matt lifted his head from the desk. She called him capable! Something warm and tender stirred within him, and then without warning, she whacked him with a ruler, and the delicious feeling evaporated.

Academically he excelled when he chose to do the work. Unfortunately, there was an inexplicable pull somewhere within him to defy rules and authority figures. When no one was watching, he felt compelled to see what he could get away with. He was a rule-tester and focused his energies on finding every possible loophole, scoffing at the mild punishments and finding little motivation or energy left for actual schoolwork most days. Under Henry's tutelage he improved his ability to swipe almost anything of value, and while he didn't pull good grades, he felt confident that he was smart enough to get away with the important things in life. Henry claimed to have never set foot in a church, especially not a Catholic one, not even a Baptist one, and never would. Matt nodded in agreement that the only purpose of a church was to make people follow a bunch of pointless rules and get money from them to boot.

"The nuns are f****** b*tches!" Dan said to Mary, putting his feet on the kitchen table and lobbing an empty pudding cup toward the garbage where it tapped the edge before clanging to the floor.

"Promise me you'll mind tomorrow!" Mary crumpled an empty cigarette pack and handed it to Matt to throw away. She looked severely from Matt to Dan, and when neither answered, she left the room in a huff, shaking her head in disgust and releasing a stream of smoke through pursed lips. The problems Mary faced had begun as a trickle and widened to a gush. Business slowed at the café. Tom's hours were cut. Her tips shriveled. Bills piled up and the rent increased. She had to make sure Matt wore long sleeves to school to cover the bruises. Tom constantly took his anger out on one of them physically.

"Hit me again, and I'll leave your skinny ass!" Mary threatened him one morning. The last thing she needed was her boys having trouble at school. Securing them a place at this private school where they could learn discipline and have structure was a rare, proud moment for Mary. "You need to be around nice kids and stay away from them good-for-nothing criminals you associate with," she pleaded with the boys before heading out to the South Town Lounge to meet some friends.

Matt stood a head taller than his peers, looming like a giant oak in a grove of seedlings. Nurture taught him to always take advantage of the upper hand, so now it was finally his turn to use both physical stature and intimidation to bully his classmates but always out of sight of the teachers. He'd have been considered the class prankster if his antics hadn't crossed the line into sadistic stunts. Anything that made someone else the brunt of a joke was fair game. A kick in the rear was a good standby, but his favorite was the underwear snuggie on a classmate in the restroom. He forcefully pulled the victim's underwear up the butt crack then repeatedly yanked at the underwear until the unsuspecting boy screamed in pain. Sifting out the easy targets became a near compulsion. The satisfaction he received from humiliating another human being was so short-lived that he was in constant search of a new victim.

The following day Dan sat hunched in his seat using a ruler to hurl spitballs at an especially annoying boy who had such good posture it pained Dan to look at him. He usually followed the rules when the nun was watching, which was often since she clipped around the room like a guard overseeing prisoners. He waited until she started explaining something on a map at the back of the room. But she snuck up behind him, stopped mid-sentence, jerked the wooden ruler from his grip, and smacked it across his hand. *Crack! Crack!*

Dan didn't falter. He leaped to his feet and snatched the ruler back. "You old b*tch! You hit me again, and I'll bash your head in!" he shouted, giving her a shove and nearly sending the crickity nun crashing into a wall. Her weathered face fell into a grimace of despair knowing that her fierce desire to help this ungodly boy was not enough to bridge the gap between what Dan needed and what she could provide. The following weekend, there was the incident of the brothers vandalizing the school windows that ended in a high-speed chase with the cops. After that, the scholarships and Mary's hope for their future disappeared under the weight of anger and hatred. The boys were shuffled back to Iles Elementary.

Then the problems closed in on Mary. After waking up with yet another black eye, she left Tom and filed for divorce. With little income, she had no way to support the three of them. By the end of the first week, she didn't even have enough money to wash their clothes—the few she'd taken when leaving Tom—at the Laundromat. Mary sheepishly handed Matt some hand-me-downs. She'd traded some of her romance novels for a bag of boy's clothes with a waitress at work. There were two pairs of worn pants, and when Matt got to school, he inconspicuously slid his legs under the desk and kept them there so no one could see the patches on the knees. He made sure not to finish all his work so that he'd be kept in at recess or the other kids would surely call him "rag bag" or "Mr. Hand-Me-Down."

Compounding the financial problems was the fact that both boys, though still in elementary school, already had an extensive history of trouble with the law. Mary cursed both God and the devil when Dan narrowly escaped a second charge of grand theft. He would never have had the close call if he'd brought the motorcycle right to Henry rather than giving in to the urge to open the throttle on a straightaway. She made the decision to send them to live with a foster family.

Chapter 12
Glimmers of Good

Matt's stomach rumbled. Dan slouched next to him on the couch. Neither of them had eaten any breakfast yet since there was no food in the house, which accounted for the scowl on Dan's face. Once again they'd be responsible for either stealing or conniving their next meal. Matt ran his fingers over the worn fabric, and this stirred up a comforting response in light of Mary's next words.

"I love you both more than you know, but you're stealing, breaking the law, and not thinking of anyone but yourselves. The devil has his hold on you, and maybe this will break it. We'll be back together as soon as you get straightened out, and I find us a place to live."

Matt protested all day, but Mary stood firm. He tried controlling the situation with anger and after that with indifference, but neither worked on Mary this time. She was uncharacteristically resolved in her decision to send them away, and this willingness to push him off onto strangers worried Matt. If there was something he truly feared, it was the unknown. What would these foster people be like? Would they be strict and uncaring like the nuns at Catholic school? Would they be uninterested like Tom's relatives whom they'd visited briefly last summer, or like the neighbors who lived on either side of them who shouted obscenities at Matt when no one else was around to hear it? Whatever lay ahead, life had already taught him that the unknown rarely turned out to be anything good.

Jack and Judy were a young couple, he a coal miner and she a stay-at-home mom, both bursting with desire to transform the lives of their first foster children, two rule-challenged, rough-edged boys who arrived at their freshly scrubbed home with its expensive—the boys couldn't believe it—*color* television. The couple sported gleaming smiles to match their manicured lawn and spotless furnishings. Matt and Dan traveled forty miles to get here, but as the week sped along, they experienced the perplexing feeling of having journeyed to a parallel planet; one with functional parents. Judy served home-cooked meals on real plates. Jack helped them with their homework every evening, taught them how to work through challenging math problems without giving up, and explained the importance of saving their allowance for future purchases. Weekends were spent at a sparkling horseshoe-shaped lake where the boys got their first taste of hot dogs roasted over a campfire and fought over the top bunk in the camper. Saturdays were spent fishing and hiking. Order and security prevailed throughout the week. Nights were quiet; no squealing tires, sirens, or cat fights to serenade the dark. "This is awesome," Matt said to Dan, lifting the edge of a fish they'd been trusted to cook over a fire they'd both helped to build.

Aside from occasional phone calls and visits with Mary, they had been apart for so long that one day Matt realized he hadn't thought about his mom all week. After a year, Jack and Judy's consistent order and kindness began to sink into the boys' bones. During this time, Mary divorced Tom and was prepared to take the boys back. "I can hardly sleep at night knowing you'll be home soon!" Mary's voice trilled into the phone. Matt didn't answer, focusing instead on the breath that had rushed from his lungs leaving him woozy.

"Are you excited to come back and live at home again?"

"Will Tom be there?"

"No, he's—"

"Sure. I'm happy."

Tom left and the boys arrived, somewhat downhearted as they'd grown to enjoy their foster family. Mary lurched through each day aimlessly with downcast eyes. It was like watching an accident happen in slow motion. Both boys noticed it. She put on a brave front, proud of the apartment she secured for them though it was small yet cluttered with her bottomless supply of books and knickknacks. Even her voice seemed to be grasping for strength, like a bulb flickering its last light before giving one final spark and dying out. She hadn't yet figured out how to function without Tom. Mary wavered, but a waitress friend stubbornly refused to let her wallow and second-guess. She took Mary to a seedy nightclub, the South Town Lounge, which bustled with action every night of the week.

These nights out increased in number and intensity in direct relation to the regrets Mary had about leaving Tom. Mary still considered him a misunderstood waif who was teased and bullied as a child and now acted tough to cover up the pain. He just needed some polishing like their secondhand table with its scratches and dents that he'd broken in another fit of anger before moving out. At least Tom had helped with some of the worries like raising two boys and making ends meet. Already she was behind in paying bills, the water company had sent a final notice, the refrigerator was always empty, and now the boys needed shoes. She didn't feel like the same person she'd been with Tom. Neither did the boys though.

For Matt and Dan, coming back to a home without Tom was almost as good as being with Jack and Judy. The boys could deal with the skimpy meals. They simply watched each other's back and took turns shoplifting snacks from the grocery store or invited themselves over to friends' houses for meals. Matt could sleep through the night. He didn't worry about Tom unleashing his anger on whoever was within striking distance at the moment his temper unfurled. Matt couldn't remember the last time he'd walked into the house without his stomach clenching. After a couple of weeks, the three of them had fallen into a comfortable routine, or so Matt thought. There was a lingering doubt that the other shoe was about to fall. Although initially elated to have her boys back, Mary reverted to either moping around the house or staying out all night with her friend. Something was off, and Matt sensed it.

Within weeks Tom and Mary were back together and soon fell into a similar routine as before. Fighting, yelling, and broken furniture. Matt would often awake to drunken bickering and knickknacks clattering against the wall at 2 AM. His anger deepened. The boys were back on the streets, slipping into their old ways with the criminal friends who welcomed them back with open arms. The lessons Jack and Judy had lovingly bestowed upon them slid away like dripping sweat in the summer sun.

After outrunning three boys who'd chased him home after school shouting threats to cut off his white b****, he arrived home assuming it would be empty. It nearly was, but not in the way he expected. The living room was barren except for the couch and a long coffee table Tom hadn't yet broken. Two cardboard boxes stood in the middle of the room, one with a crushed corner and both labeled "LIVING ROOM" with black marker across the front. Void of furnishings, the dingy carpet revealed a patchwork of stains from wall to wall that they had never noticed. Dishes were clattering in the kitchen when Tom suddenly appeared in the doorway looking sweaty. Sweatier than usual.

"Pack up," he barked, nodding to Matt to head upstairs, which he immediately did.

Matt raced up the steps to the floating sound of Mary complaining to Tom just before the back door slammed. "Damn. I have two kids who delivered newspapers, but I can't find enough paper to wrap eight glasses." Dan was already in the bedroom stuffing the contents of a dresser drawer into a garbage bag.

"Damn, woman. You got boxes of old newspapers." Tom's muffled voice radiated through the furnace vent.

"Those are my good papers, Tom. The ones I'm saving for the articles in them."

Matt opened the door to a half-packed room.

"We're moving," Dan said, kicking a roll of plastic bags in Matt's direction. "Anything you wanna take you better bag up. I ain't packing any of your crap for you."

"Where we going?"

Dan paused and stared vacantly at a bundle of semi-clean clothes he was preparing to stuff into a bag before letting it fall to his side. "South Dakota. Tom got a job there."

Dan rattled wordlessly around the room, and Matt tossed some clothes into a bag before working up the nerve to ask Dan, "Are you glad we're moving?"

Dan snorted. "We live in a sh**hole, and today three spooks called me a cracker and chased me down a back street." He tipped his head to reveal a fresh bruise on his jawline. "So, yeah, I'm sure this new city will be just dandy."

Matt's mom, Mary Barr, in her younger days—headstrong and optimistic. This small-town girl yearned for the Big City lights and eventually moved to Saint Louis, and then Chicago.

Matt (age 9) at the time of his first high-speed chase with the police.

Chapter 13
Midwest Menace

Compared to Springfield, the city of Sioux Falls, South Dakota, seemed like Shangri-La. It boasted a population of 72,500 in 1970, making it the largest city in the state. Nestled in the southeast corner of the state where it bumped shoulders with Minnesota and Iowa, it was known for the cascading falls along the Big Sioux River and was a popular stopping point for vacationers heading to the Black Hills. Lush parks and low crime in this nearly all-white city seemed to be everything they desired. It was the crown jewel as far as South Dakota cities go. Dan entered a state-of-the-art high school in this land of manicured lawns and new school clothes purchased from the mall which had recently opened on the edge of the city.

But the city had pockets of poverty, seedy bars, and rough edges. It was these unsavory areas with their potential for exploitation that claimed Matt before he even had time to hang the Cowboys football posters on his bedroom wall. At twelve years old and just on the cusp of puberty, Matt would soon discover that Sioux Falls provided the perfect breeding ground for someone with a criminal mindset and a quick temper to fester over the next several years.

Mary and Tom separated as soon as the move to Sioux Falls was complete. Tom quickly tired of this replay of the family life, so he slithered away to another town. For some reason, in a new setting Mary seemed to bounce back faster. Perhaps it was the tangible goodness of the place. It didn't take long for any of them to realize that the hatefulness and prejudice that had colored their lives in Springfield lived somewhere only at the far edges of this city.

Mary collapsed onto the unbroken side of the couch and allowed herself a small smile of self-satisfaction. Her boys were now settled in a homespun Midwestern town where they were certain to meet plenty of good kids the way they had back in foster care and Catholic school. Mary didn't realize that although the physical move was over, Matt's penchant for criminal activity kept him rooted to the bowels of Springfield. A brokenness within him continued to draw him down the dismal path of incarceration no matter where he lived. Mary convinced herself they'd all move forward with a new life that included plenty of responsibility for her boys.

"There's a real nice lady down the street," she told Matt and Dan, setting plates of meatloaf and mashed potatoes before them at the Formica table pushed too far toward the door in order to accommodate the piles of cardboard boxes still waiting to be unpacked. She took it as a good omen when the lady walked over to introduce herself and then spent an hour having coffee and talking. After living here only a few weeks, Mary met a neighbor who was also raising two boys on her own, though they were younger, six and nine.

"She's just like me in thinking kids need responsibility." Mary looked at her boys sternly from the open refrigerator where she was rummaging around for a bottle of ketchup. "I know I packed ketchup. It was a new bottle ..." She closed the door and began searching through the nearest box while Dan and Matt waited at the table; Dan flung a spoonful of potato at Matt, who smacked it onto the floor. "Have you seen that ketchup in any of these boxes?" The boys shrugged. "Here it is!" She hoisted the bottle onto the table and then wiped potato off the floor with her napkin and went in search of a garbage bag.

"I was saying, she believes in kids learning responsibility. So—"

"You're beating that drum again?" Dan rolled his eyes at the jolt of that word he despised so much, *responsibility*.

Mary continued, "*So,* one of you is going to babysit for her boys this Saturday. She's going on a date. Lord knows she deserves a night out."

"Matt will. He doesn't have a life," Dan said, giving his brother a shove, "and I'm going out with my friends," Dan left the room with Mary shouting after him.

"Going where?" she yelled while carrying his plate over to the sink.

Dan didn't answer.

"Where ya going on Saturday?"

"Out."

"Out with who?"

"Nobody you know."

"Well, bring whoever it is here. I want to meet them." There was a pause, so she waited expectantly for an answer, not even breathing.

Dan rolled his eyes, slammed the front door, and left.

Mary turned to Matt and gestured with both arms as if to say, *Well, that settles it. You're it!* Matt didn't disagree, so Mary let out a throaty laugh and patted him on the back. Between Catholic school, the foster home, and this move, at least one of her boys was turning it around.

On Saturday night Mary stood on the front steps to make sure Matt went straight to the neighbor's house; she had generously promised to pay him fifty cents an hour. Mary locked the door, out of habit, and poured herself another cup of coffee from the nearly empty pot. She unpacked four boxes and rearranged the ceramic angels just so before retiring on the sofa with a romance novel. An involuntary smile crossed her face. Hope settled gently on her lips. She had a new job at a convenience store, Dan had made new friends already, though she wasn't sure whether that was a good thing or not, and Matt was earning money down the street the honest way. This move was the best thing that had happened to them since she'd hooked up the Catholic school scholarship, which should have been a good thing had the nun not overreacted. Mary felt such an upsurge of happiness that she flicked on *The Mary Tyler Moore Show* and then pulled out the laundry bag and began ironing a week's worth of blouses. When the phone rang at 10:30 PM, her stomach coiled.

"Ma'am, we booked your son into the facility tonight for stealing an automobile. We need someone to come down here." It was the juvenile detention center. Mary sickened at the knowledge that Dan was right back to thieving. Her heart was full of trust for just about everyone except her son's friends. She knew he had been racing around on a friend's motorcycle. Hell, just a few days ago he tore right out of the driveway right in front of her and roared down the street with some new friend cheering him on. The next time she managed to corner him, Mary bent his ear, telling him that someday he would pay the price for his recklessness.

Brittle darkness settled onto the now empty street in front of the detention center, a much more modern building than the one in Illinois, she noted. After being buzzed in by a gum-smacking girl barely in her twenties, an annoyingly cheerful young man, a college student she deduced, led her into a small office to sign papers. She was ready to lay into Dan again about paying the price when the worker shocked her by telling her that it was Matt who was in their custody. Then the story unfolded. After Matt put the two boys to bed, he called a friend over, and on the spur of the moment, the two of them got a whim to take the lady's car for a couple of hours of joy riding, intending to return before she got home. Unfortunately, while Matt's penchant for speed often worked to his advantage when outrunning the law, tonight was not one of those times. While racing the vehicle through a residential area, at speeds beyond what a twelve-year-old car thief could control, he rounded an unfamiliar curve and crashed into a parked pickup, totaling both vehicles.

"We're required to detain him until Monday when he can appear in front of a juvenile court judge, but we have some preliminary paperwork that needs to be endorsed by you tonight," the college kid explained, in what Mary felt was an attempt to use unnecessarily big words to intimidate her.

"He's twelve years old!" she countered.

"He's a twelve-year-old who will likely be charged with grand theft, ma'am."

The following week Matt had his first of what was to become numerous encounters with the South Dakota court system. He was put on probation and assigned a parole officer to check on his behavior each week. "You're going to kill yourself one of these days! Look what happens when you let the devil get you!" Mary tried appealing to his sense of reason. "You just made a new friend, and now *poof!*" She gestured, bringing both hands above her head in outward arcs to indicate that everything good had just disappeared. Matt knew it hadn't. He wasn't even rattled by the experience. He continued as if nothing happened; he just had to learn to be sneakier and more careful about his criminal exploits.

Mary was wrong to worry about Matt losing this friend. The boy bragged about his exploits with Matt to a circle of wide-eyed twelve-year-olds who could think of no better responses than *whoa* or *that's crazy* while giving sideways glances, unsure if they were being fed a bunch of bull. It didn't take long for these boys to learn that any wild story circulating about Matt was likely a true one. He was tall and athletic enough that after school one day he pounded a boy three years older than himself in spite of starting out by getting sucker punched. This bloody fight behind one of the churches across from Whittier Junior High, a sprawling two-story brick structure in one the city's oldest neighborhoods, clinched his reputation as the kid to be feared. Matt's impulsiveness shrouded his attentive nature; he habitually learned from others, taking notes.

Especially when someone made a mistake. Following this fight, he made sure he was the one sucker punching, but only when the odds against him were impossible.

Whenever Matt entered a room, the atmosphere changed. Something almost tangible sparked in the air. There was something alive just below his skin that worked like a magnet, either pulling close or repelling those around him. Most of the boys realized where they stood in the junior high pecking order and either chose to be in Matt's circle, if they had a wild streak, or kept a wide berth and avoided eye contact. He found other kids willing to cut classes with him or not go to school at all. In Springfield, he was the brunt of the bullying, and now as one of the biggest kids in the school, he was ready to give it back. He honed in on pointing out others' unwanted physical features and fought readily with the slightest provocation. When Mary moved them to a different part of town, Matt refused to change schools and kept going to Whittier where he had made friends. He even pulled good grades in science once he discovered it was interesting.

"I'm not going to Patrick Henry with those rich p******," he told Mary, referring to the newest junior high. Now a 190-pound ninth-grader, he was welcomed with open arms onto the wrestling team at Whittier and thrived on having a place to release his frustrations without getting in trouble. His team was the closest he came to feeling part of a real family besides the year he spent with Jack and Judy. He showed up for every practice and even found he didn't mind following orders from the coach, something that surprised even Matt. But when the season was over, he went back to fighting on the street.

"You got expelled for fighting again, Matt. They're not letting you back. This is what happens when you mouth off to teachers and let the devil tempt you. Maybe you'll learn now," Mary said, wringing her hands and having no way of knowing Matt would turn in his wrestling gear and never go back.

Chapter 14
A Snitch in Time

"Matt the Man, the Leader of the Land is uncatchable!" He razzed Dan, punching him in the arm a few times. At fifteen, Matt now stood level with Dan and outweighed him by a few pounds. "While you've been wasting your time slaving away at the Western Steak House for a few bucks a night, I've learned what few have ever been able to accomplish: how to beat the system!"

"You haven't accomplished s**t. You're a petty little street rat who has to borrow his mom's car to steal a sixty-dollar grill 'cuz you don't got your own ride."

Matt seethed, especially because he knew Dan was right. Dan was roaring around the city and cruising the downtown loop on weekend nights participating in games of chicken on a fairly respectable Triumph motorcycle while Matt had nothing. It was time to up the ante. Bring his thievery to a new level. A more lucrative level. An idea planted itself in his head on a seductive June afternoon as Matt just happened to be walking past the Shadco Honda Dealership on the east side of the city. Sitting out in front were twenty-five decked out motorcycles gleaming in the sun. The manager had just moved them to the front of the lot to entice customers to take a look at the irresistible beasts. Matt strolled over to take a look. Surprisingly, the keys were in the ignition of each cycle, and he could not resist. The thought exploded from an idea into a compulsion. Matt inspected the motorcycles as if browsing while keeping a keen eye out for the right opportunity. The second the salesman became distracted, Matt began swiftly pushing a bright red 750 motocross bike down the block until he was completely out of sight. He hopped aboard, kick-started it to life, and went roaring down a side street. He didn't have much experience with a bike this powerful.

The bike responded easily to the subtle turns of his body, allowing him to accelerate with each successive bend it the road, challenging not only his reflexes but his threshold for the extreme. At the edge of the city, he burst onto a county road, cranked full throttle, and strained forward, waiting for the rush of adrenaline that he knew wouldn't come until he'd surpassed his previous record for speed. The wind whipped strands of hair across his face as he pushed forward, veering around the occasional car and refusing to slow down. When the speedometer finally crept past 75 mph, the tension peaked, and a thrill spread through him like hot water shooting through a thermal geyser. He was addicted to the thrill of danger.

After a few hours of recklessly tearing around the city, Matt found himself back in the Shadco neighborhood. He'd stopped at a pay phone to call a couple of houses where he could bring this stolen prize, but no one was around. He couldn't bring the bike home under Mary's watchful eye, so he made the split-second decision to return it to the lot. The flush from speeding had faded, and he was ready for another challenge, he reasoned; he'd return the bike, dusty but unblemished, as stealthily as he'd taken it. The pathetic white-collars would never even know what had transpired under their untrained eyes.

Later, Matt would use critical mistakes he'd made as a lesson to improve his skills in scoring goods. He'd already built a reputation in this neighborhood. *Enlarge my territory.* A salesman had seen him lurking around and soon after noticed an empty space where a motocross bike should have been. *Make sure they can't identify me. Never make returns once the property is in hand.* Yet each heist had a new set of circumstances and what he learned from one mistake wasn't applicable to the next situation, so largely he forgot about his failures and focused on the successes.

Mary sat off to the side of the dark-paneled juvenile courtroom looking small and powerless beneath the cavernous ceiling. That morning she'd insisted Matt look presentable, so now here he sat tugging at the top button of a long-sleeved dress shirt she'd picked up at the Goodwill. They'd argued about it with Matt insisting the judge wouldn't make a decision based on whether he showed up wearing jeans and a T-shirt or these uncomfortable p**** clothes.

Up to this point, Matt had received the proverbial slap on the hand and assumed that as a fifteen-year-old he'd be cut some slack for a few more years. He showed up prepared for community service or more probation, but the seasoned judge was not so lenient this time.

"You've used up all your chances. You don't get any more. Matthew Lofton, I hereby sentence you to the South Dakota State Training School in Plankinton, South Dakota, for a term to be determined by the staff." Matt's heart pounded. He no longer felt like Matt the Man.

"Have you ever been to Plankinton?" He called a friend from his junior high school the next day, trying to sound casual. The boy gasped and said no. Even Matt's school friends who ran on the rough side hadn't crossed a line beyond occasional shoplifting. Matt was eons ahead of other high school students in terms of illegal activities. Nobody he asked even knew of someone who'd been to Plankinton, and Matt found himself quickly sinking into a depression. He didn't fear much, but he feared the unknown.

The state training school towered over the small town of Plankinton. Anchored by an intimidating four-story fortress blemished by crumbling mortar and block, there were several

71

outlying cottages as well on this surprisingly fenceless campus. Matt was assigned to a building with dorms laid out military style, each containing ten bunk beds to house some of the 250 boys and 50 girls at the school. The dismal interior was laced with rusty pipes that ran the length of the institutionally bland walls. For a thrill-seeker used to unlimited freedom and fast motorcycle rides down the open highway, the days soon stretched as endless as the South Dakota prairie on which the school sat.

"What do you have to do to get out of this place?" Matt whispered in the dark of night to the boy in the next bed. Two days in and he already felt cagey.

There was a pause. "W-Why would you ask that?" the boy asked with an unsettling concern in his voice.

"What the hell? So I can figure out what the game is to get out of here."

Matt's eyes had adjusted to the dark, and he could see an outline of the boy turn away onto his side. The room shrank back, leaving only the forlorn sounds of suppressed sniffles that rose and faded against the colorless gloom. Around the sleeping area, formerly white tiles, now cracked and faded to yellow, did their best to gleam following an afternoon scrubbing with Pine-Sol, and some unidentifiable institutional odor mingled with the cold brick walls to conjure the most unwelcome of smells. Matt's breath caught painfully in his sinuses. The shock of being banished from society cracked his bravado, and the strong front he'd worn throughout the day fell like chunks from a battered wall. He was going into this battle against *the man*, as he'd heard someone here call it, blind, alone, and unprepared.

With no ally to guide him on the ins and outs of Plankinton, Matt labored to figure out the system on his own, but not without a few dire consequences. Unaccustomed to being watched or found out, Matt was caught off-guard during the first session of group which was held three times each week. During group, ten surly boys sat in a circle, all eager to exploit each other's weaknesses in exchange for their own freedom. It was a game of survival, and only the unscrupulous could win. Dave, a short, heavyset man with a zealous streak of redneck, goaded the kids to rat on each other. It was a snitch session. Everyone was expected to give his life history, admit his problems, and tell if anyone else had screwed up. At the end of group, the ragtag group of criminals, misfits, and psychopaths was granted the power to vote and help determine if anyone was rehabilitated and ready to leave the school.

During Matt's first group session, the other members turned on him immediately, knowing his lack of familiarity with the process would mean the heat would probably stay off of them for the night.

"I would like to bring to the group Matt's authority figure problem," a kid from West River, South Dakota, chirped in a grating voice that almost brought Matt to his feet. The boy had a bright red birthmark on the side of his neck and cheek.

"I've noticed the same thing that Cherry has," another boy added. What Matt noticed was an eagerness here to attach derogatory names based on physical differences. It was a cornerstone of the cracking he learned in Springfield, and the tendency to use any weak point to peck away at someone else's bravado came naturally to him.

"Go ahead and explain your point." Group leader Dave shot Cherry an encouraging look and leaned forward, resting his arms atop his chunky legs for support.

"Well, last night Matt was telling us that staff member Lori was a first class b*tch who doesn't know crap."

Dave narrowed his eyes with a bogus look of concern before directing his attention to Matt.

"It sounds like you have an anger problem, Matt. Why does staff member Lori make you angry when she's only doing her job?"

And then Matt made a series of errors that he would repeat at several sessions before catching on to the hidden rules of group.

"I don't have an anger problem." Matt scowled. The boys in the group snorted and shook their heads at each other with knowing looks. Matt had taken the bait. The newcomers always did.

"Let's have a show of hands. Who thinks Matt has an anger problem?"

Almost every hand went up.

Dave continued, "The group thinks you have an anger problem, Matt. Do you think they're all wrong?"

"Yeah, because I don't have an anger problem." Matt sat back assuredly, not caring if any of these losers thought he had a problem, which he didn't.

"But you said that staff member Lori is a b*tch. That's anger, Matt," Dave said to a chorus of nods from the others.

"She is a b*tch. I'm not the angry one, you are," Matt added, pointing to Dave's mouth cramp. The leader's face pulsed red whenever Matt didn't agree with him.

"Matt also told us that you're an irritable jerk who hates kids," another boy added.

Within minutes, Dave was pushed past his limit and jumped to his feet yelling. "Matt! Listen to me! You need to admit you have an anger problem! You're holding the whole group back!"

Matt responded with a smirky shake of his head and arms crossed over his chest.

"THAT'S IT! I'M NOT TAKING ANY MORE OF THIS! YOU'RE GOING TO LOCKUP!"

Lockup was a solitary cell. A toilet and a sink. Bare walls staring him down around the clock. He stayed there for a couple of days, allowed out only once to walk down the hall for a shower where a meager stream dribbled lukewarm water on his oily scalp. When his hair finally dried, the unrinsed soap film bonded strands of hair together, leaving his hair feeling dirtier than before. Matt finger-combed the strands into obedience, fully aware that no one could see him in lockup but still concerned about his appearance. Worst of all, lockup meant no trip to the canteen for a movie and a Coke on the weekend, the only bright spot in this soulless institution. The food served in the hole tasted terrible, and the isolation hobbled a piece of his heart. Matt cursed himself for tripping up as much as he cursed the system that trapped him here. It was another reminder not to trust anyone. The boys from his group turned on him with relish in hopes of increasing their own chances of moving up the ladder. Cherry had the intelligence of a laundry basket, yet he managed to get Matt stuck in this micro-hellhole.

The strain of living in this den of violence only intensified situations that could have otherwise been deescalated through properly trained staff. Instead, kids were nudged into explosive fits then wrestled to the floor and cuffed ankles to hands before being hauled off to the hole. Matt's rage eventually diminished during his time in the hole, though his hatred for authority swelled, and he got out in a few days. However, his volcanic temper earned him a return trip a week later for the same mistakes. The second time in, isolation became emotionally painful. Pain turned to anger, anger turned to hate, and hate turned to aggression. No one cared if he kicked, screamed, or hurled insults. Segregation from the others at Plankinton had seemed almost unbearable before, and now freedom withered to an illusion. Matt was a wanderer, a free spirit with a restless core. The confines of the tiny cell seemed more paralyzing than when Dan would come up behind him and cover Matt's mouth and nose with clenched hands, laughing as Matt twisted and convulsed until he eventually escaped. He was resourceful, too. So he did the only thing he could; think. Contemplate. Analyze. When his body was forced into confinement, his mind made up for it by transforming into a cunning machine. In the hostile silence, he noticed a pattern of who got released from the center, who was successful. It was the kids who admitted their problems. He realized it was a game with no winners, and Matt had no qualms about playing the system. He would admit he had problems with anger, authority, and stealing if it would get him out of here. *Why not,* he reasoned without even a flutter of shame. He quickly learned to thrive in the dysfunctional atmosphere and stealthily entered the blame game. He quickly deduced that Dave was unqualified yet ambitious. A poor combination that fortunately made it easy for Matt to beat him at his own game. He returned to his group feeling infinitely wiser.

"It ticked me off when Matt rolled his eyes at you today when you told him to remake his bed," Cherry blurted out to Dave as soon as group began.

"Matt, respect of authority figures is expected at all times. What do you have to say for yourself?" Dave, with his piggy eyes and fake look of concern, was relatively calm because he hadn't had a chance to get worked up yet.

Matt seethed inside, yet forced himself to nod in agreement. "I guess I was having a bad day, and I was wrong to roll my eyes. I realize that you only asked me to remake my bed because I hadn't done it right the first time. I have a lot of respect for the way you're helping me improve, and I wish Cherry felt the same way about staff member Lori and hadn't acted like he was going to punch her when her back was turned." Now the heat was off Matt and on Cherry instead. *Game point!* He imagined smashing his fist into Cherry's face.

Immediately, someone accused the boy to Matt's left of stealing, and the rest of the group ganged up on the kid like starving hyenas. After some heated verbal rumbles, the boy kicked back his chair and blasted the snitch with a right fist across the nose. This time it was someone else being hauled off to the hole, and the whole

76

dysfunctional scene repeated itself in some variation three times a week, every week, during group.

When they weren't in group berating and ratting on each other, they were expected to work together like a family. Otherwise, the other members voted that the person was holding the group back. Dave handed his charges each an orange vest, and they set out to pick up litter. None of them would have agreed to this, but the payoff was a few hours in the canteen on the weekend and occasionally a movie in town. There wasn't a fence around the building like at a prison, so their group leader kept a close eye on them. But really, and they all discussed this at length, where would they go?

"All you have to do is kiss ass," Matt said, swishing the basketball through the hoop, "and tell them what they want to hear, and it's easy to get out." At the canteen one weekend, he confided this to Calvin, easily the only person at Plankinton Matt intuitively trusted. For one thing, Calvin refused to rat on anyone.

"Screw them. I'm not admitting problems I don't have. I'm not narcing on anyone either. They ain't gonna break me. I have standards," Calvin said, though he desperately wanted to leave the place.

One weekend Calvin didn't show up at the canteen, and Matt heard it was because he was in the hole. During a group activity, Calvin and a friend snuck away and ran off through the cornfields that surrounded the little town. They walked all night long and hardly stopped to rest. They figured they were far enough away from the training school that no one would be looking for them, so they went onto a blacktop road and started hitchhiking.

"There's never a cop around when you need one, but they're always there when you don't!" one of them had commented while racing back through the cornfields after spotting a highway patrol car pulling up behind them. The patrolman called for backup, and the boys were soon cornered and brought back to Plankinton.

77

After a week in the hole, the group leader accused Calvin of "not being on board." Everyone was expected to admit his problems, whether it was anger, stealing, lying, or authority problems. Pretty much all of the boys here had all of those problems, but the world handed them pain, so the only way they knew how to survive was to fight back hard. After all, the whole world was against them. Before getting released, a resident had to reach reality level by admitting his problems. Prior to that, there were levels for developing self-control and tolerance, getting involved in the lives of others in the group, and having respect for authority. At the end of group, the dysfunctional circle of thugs would vote to help determine if anyone was rehabilitated and ready to leave the school.

Calvin stayed at the school upholding his standards for two years until he turned eighteen, and the staff was required to let him out. Not only was he unrehabilitated, but he had become a more skilled criminal as well. Just over a year after arriving, Matt learned the game so well he was released. He left Plankinton with a strong distaste for snitches, a trait he considered more loathsome than weakness.

Chapter 15
Night Shift

Dan stole a case of beer from the back of a delivery truck and in the safety of his bedroom grudgingly shared this wealth with Matt, knowing he could use this act of kindness for future favors.

"I won't forget my generosity the next time I need to borrow money from you or something," he said, reminding Matt of the implicit strings-attached agreement that accompanied any favor. Dan wiped his generous nose with a napkin then lobbed it at Matt.

"F*** you, Karl Malden. I gave you that pair of jeans last week that don't fit me no more. We're even." At age sixteen, he had now caught up to Dan in size.

Dan paused and then noticed a newly empty spot on the wall. "Where's your Cowboys poster?"

"I don't like them anymore. I'm a Steelers fan."

"That's appropriate. Steal us a bottle of bourbon from that liquor store." He motioned down the street, "You about drank up all this beer. You can go out with your big owl eyes tonight and see what else you can find us."

The dysfunctional accounting session of petty favors continued until Matt raised both hands skyward and declared himself "the cracking victor." The brotherly exchanges grew more civil once they were at eye level, yet they also didn't see each other much. Dan had girlfriends now, though Matt considered each one nastier than the last and assigned each girl an offensive name that he wasn't afraid to utter in her presence. Usually, his brother was off somewhere with a girl, which suited Matt fine since he had his own friends. He also devoted a good portion of each day to souping up a motorcycle for resale or plotting some petty scam. His biggest obstacle remained an uncontrollable temper. He hadn't always been that way. It was a remnant of ugliness that seized him back in Springfield and refused to relinquish its hold on him.

Shortly after leaving Plankinton, he was introduced to alcohol's ability to dilute the perpetual anger that simmered just beneath his skin. The effects were deceptive, though, and he realized that. Beer didn't eliminate his anger; in fact, it created a tempest of its own that usually led to fistfights. It offered momentary relief from the raw memories filled with injustice that got his head pounding at the slightest trigger. Alcohol was a poor companion for someone who operated by impulses that had no logical origin. With a booze-induced confidence, he left the house and strolled down familiar streets and unfamiliar alleys until he was nearly back home. The sight of a garage's side door ajar lured him with the temptation of a Greek Siren. He crept into the darkened garage and rummaged around the contents until landing upon an item that brought a smile to his face and eventually put a lot of money in his pocket. It was a set of bolt cutters.

****

Matt waited until he was confident that Mary was asleep before slipping his bedroom window open with feathery hands as a sort of self-competition in stealthiness, though Mary likely would have slept through clatter. It was a game he developed to hone his skills; seeing what he could get away with even when nothing was at stake. It served another purpose as well. Deep inside him, a battle ensued — the arrogance of a young street criminal versus the reality of law and order. By now he had the attitude that he could get away with anything, and this translated into a powerful mindset of fearlessness. Instead of learning from his mistakes, he tended to just forget about them. He glided out of the window with the keys to Mary's car and the bolt cutters in hand and headed to a previously scouted stylish brick house several blocks away. In the middle of the night, people were sleeping deeply, or upon hearing a sound preferred to convince themselves they'd heard a car door, or that it was the out-of-control teenager down the street just getting home from a night of revelry.

Snip. The bolt cutters sliced through the thick metal, and the padlock dropped to the ground with a clank before Matt could catch it, sending the dog next door into a raucous frenzy. Matt ducked behind the twelve-foot fishing boat and paused. *Nope, the fools are all asleep.* He reassured himself that in the dead of night, a noise back here in the alley only sounded loud because he was right next to it but was inaudible to someone not even awake. With the dog still barking furiously in the background, he lifted the six-horsepower Mercury motor from the boat's stern and hoisted it into the trunk of Mary's beat-up Plymouth Satellite. Matt drove down the alley smirking. He was certain the money he'd pocketed over the weekend rivaled that of some of the snobby, candy-assed classmates who coasted off bloated allowances from daddy. He fenced the motor for a quick Benjamin from one of the older guys Dan associated with. Mary never knew he left at 3 AM to work his forty-minute "night shift."

This preference for corruption set him apart from most other students at Lincoln High School, which took in the city's more affluent and middle-class students along with a small percentage of low-income Eastsiders. Matt's ceaseless hunt for the next crime, the next heist, the next swindle, was his oxygen. This was what life was about: con or be conned. Life was whatever you could grab from it. The games at Plankinton and the games in the real world were no match for his corrupt cunning.

For the next two years, Matt was able to deceive his P.O. and Mary by slyly hiding his unlawful nocturnal activities in spite of the 9 PM curfew that was part of his probation. With each heist, he honed his craft, learning from small errors and near misses. There was an occasional fistfight but nothing to alarm the authorities. Matt was able to pull adequate grades with little effort, though he was still oblivious to the extent of his intelligence. He used $75 to buy a four-door Chevy Bel Air, preferring to spend most of his illegally obtained cash on booze and pot. He continued putting the bolt cutters to work under the mask of night, accumulating boat motors, gas grills, tools, lawn mowers, and even motorcycles. When he couldn't fence his stolen goods, and they started to accumulate, he found an abandoned house or building to hide the items. His invincibility soared with each successful plunder.

Chapter 16
My Blood Type Is Mustang

When Matt turned eighteen, his juvenile court records were sealed, and he whooped inside at getting one over on the judicial system. He had a clean slate but hadn't considered what it would take to keep the record in its pristine condition. He was chained to a criminal mindset that would limit his potential for decades. Over the next few years, his criminal finesse grew in proportion to his physical attributes. A new chapter as an adult offender had just begun and wouldn't slow down until he accumulated a rap sheet of over forty arrests. Some of the heat came courtesy of a nudge from Dan, who was now living on his own on the east side of Sioux Falls.

Dan glided across the room with what he called his "street stride," a cocky strut he felt made him look tough. His feet skated along the linoleum floor while his head bobbed slightly in rhythm.

"You look like a spastic chicken." Matt sneered. He didn't really care, except that if he didn't tell Dan how stupid it looked, no one else would. It was his brotherly duty.

"You don't know nothin'. You're a lame p****," Dan shot back, unruffled.

"Okay, light bulb nose. Mr. Magoo," Matt cracked on.

"F*** you, pasty. Get some sun, so you don't look like Casper the Ghost." For some reason, Dan's voice cracked on the last words.

"Casper the Ghost," Matt repeated in a mocking-squeaky voice. "Chicken Boy can cackle, too." Matt always got the last crack, even during their many meaningless exchanges. Their brotherly bond was powerful even though it had been forged on the shared experiences of domestic abuse, shoplifting, underage drinking, and other petty crimes.

Like Dan, Matt had a toxic relationship with speed. Not the drug but the kind associated with motorcycles, cars, and women. One day, the temptation presented itself in the form of a cherry red 1966 Mustang with mag rims. Matt coveted the coy beauty that was built from the rear end to the engine for racing, with its four-speed on the floor. When he wanted something this desperately, there was little that would stop him. He dickered with the owner on the price, and then rushed to the bank to get a loan.

The loan officer penned some figures onto an official form and pushed the paper across the desk. "The vehicle is too late of a model for the amount of the loan you're requesting," the man said, his Adam's apple bobbing up and down under Matt's combative gaze.

Matt pushed the paper back to the man without glancing at it. "My mom will co-sign the loan." The man shook his head. Even with a co-signer the bank could not issue the loan. Unfortunately for Matt, time spent in Plankinton did nothing to deter his criminal mindset. In fact, it had given him time to add to his arsenal of tricks and hatch a plan that now needed just a little tweaking. The next morning, he drove past the used car lots until he spotted a 1977 Mustang priced about the same as the 1966 Mustang he really wanted. He walked in and asked to test drive this newer car, mentioning he'd stop by the bank to see if he could get a loan.

It worked. The loan officer looked over the '77 Mustang, took down the VIN, and gave Matt the loan he needed. He returned the newer car back to the car lot. By then the salesman was at lunch, so Matt handed the keys to another employee and with cash in hand went to buy the '66 cherry red marvel using the money he'd received for the '77. With the flair of a professional, he procured a loan that didn't require him to produce a title. All he had to do was make his monthly payments on the loan.

It almost worked. When the salesman returned from lunch, he saw the '77 Mustang parked back on the lot. Eager to complete a deal, the snoopy salesman called the bank and inquired as to whether a gentleman named Matt Lofton was able to secure a loan for the vehicle. The bank informed him that Matt left about an hour ago with the cash. When Matt failed to return to the dealership, the snoopy salesman called the bank again. The loan officer drove over to Matt's house and asked him why he hadn't bought the Mustang. With no time to hatch a better story, Matt explained that the salesman wasn't there, so he was going to wait until after the weekend.

"It doesn't work that way," the banker explained. "You need to give us the money back right now."

"I don't have the money. I put it in my account."

The man went back to the bank, checked Matt's account, and found that the money was not in there. When he still didn't go buy the '77 on Monday, the bank had him arrested.

Now an adult, Matt was convicted of felony grand theft and defrauding a bank.

Chapter 17
You Can't Buy Happiness, But You Can Buy Drugs

Matt spent his nineteenth and twentieth birthdays in a steel cage at the county jail. When he was released after one and a half years, Mary dropped him off at Dan's, where the Mustang was waiting for him. He did the jail time for defrauding the bank, but the terms didn't include paying back the money. He never mentioned that he had the '66 Mustang and just said he blew the money, so restitution was jail time. He peeked in the garage for a glimpse at the car and then turned the door handle to the house, but it was locked. He peered in through the window of the door, which was blocked by two yellowed curtains trimmed with brown pom poms and pulled tightly across the glass. Matt pounded on the door until a hand swept the curtains aside, and Dan's face appeared.

"Is anyone with you?" he asked, craning his neck to look behind Matt.

"Why, are you running a private country club outta here now?"

Dan opened the door far enough to peek his head through and carefully scanned the yard behind Matt as if enemy soldiers might come charging out to storm the house. Satisfied, he opened the door and quickly motioned Matt inside.

"You can't be too careful," he explained, motioning for Matt to follow him through the living room, which contained nothing but a

87

sagging brown couch and two stiff chairs placed evenly around a small television set that was balanced precariously on an undersized table.

"Did you turn into Julia Child?" Matt asked as Dan began pulling small baggies, scales, and finally a large paper bag from a locked cupboard.

Dan kept his eyes focused on a small handheld scale to which he clipped a baggie. "Watch and learn. There aren't many people I can trust so you can earn some fast cash if you aren't stupid," he said while carefully placing a small scoop of marijuana into the baggie.

Matt opened several cupboard doors until he found a bottle of Jim Beam. It had been a while since a good swig of alcohol washed over his tongue. Those who regularly frequented the jail informed Matt that while homemade hooch was available in prison, there was none to be had in jail. Unlike jail, prison inmates work in the kitchen where they can steal yeast and other ingredients. Sometimes a guy on furlough or work release smuggled in some pot and shared it with a close friend, but for the most part, they smoked it themselves or sold it for an outrageous profit. As usual, Matt took careful mental notes of the best ways to smuggle anything into this house of boredom. Who knew when he might need to do the same thing?

Fast food cups cluttered the counter, so Matt rinsed one out and poured himself a healthy serving of Jim Beam while keeping one eye on Dan, who was adding small bits of green to the bag on the scale until he was completely satisfied that he wasn't giving away any weed for free but also the buyer couldn't complain he was cheated. The burning liquid gave Matt an immediate sense of calm. A few more glasses drew out the mean inside of him but at the same time washed away the humiliation he felt over the past months when his every move was managed by some control freak with a badge who got his kicks out of dominating some down-and-out petty criminals. Since Plankinton, alcohol was his go-to after he discovered its miraculous ability to take the edge off any uncomfortable feelings, embarrassments, or other problems life was bound to hand a young adult. The booze perfected this smoke and mirror trick so well that he forgot about the problems that plagued his life since he was a kid. Although on parole, he soon began prowling the nightclubs and smoky pool halls and doing whatever felt right at the moment but thinking of consequences later.

During Matt's previous incarceration, Dan had begun charting the murky waters of the Sioux Falls drug trade. It had happened rather innocently. Dan worked long hours at a steakhouse and also tinkered with cars and motorcycles in his spare time. He came to appreciate the relaxing effects of a joint or on long days, a hit of speed. He could barely make ends meet, but with his knack for thriftiness, he quickly discovered that if he saved until he had enough to buy a few ounces of pot or several hits of speed, he could sell the extra, and in turn, pay for his own recreational drug use.

One day he showed up as usual at Stringbean's house on payday with the intention of buying a larger than usual order. Stringbean, who was shrewd, tall, and rail thin, lived just outside the city in a rundown ranch house with few neighbors to notice his busy driveway or to care about the snarling Dobermans patrolling the yard. Dan, like others who frequented this drug house, couldn't have cared less about the overgrown shrubbery bursting from the base of the house, the weed-strewn lawn, or the cracked sidewalk leading to the crumbling cement steps.

Stringbean reached for Dan's usual order and held it in his outstretched arm.

"I was thinking I'd buy a few more ounces this time if you can spare it," Dan said, holding out a wad of cash.

Stringbean hesitated and surveyed Dan with wary eyes that were trained to differentiate between a setup and a potential business venture. "How many ounces?"

"Sixteen. You got that much?"

The corner of Stringbean's mouth turned up, and he let out an amused chortle. "Yeah, I'm pretty sure I got a pound. I don't sell that much to just anyone though. My risk changes when I sell someone that quantity. Where'd you suddenly get that much money?" he asked, knowing that someone who'd gotten caught with drugs might try turning the cops onto a bigger fish in exchange for a lenient sentence. He was suspicious of anyone coming to him with a sudden windfall of cash.

"I fixed up that old Valiant and sold it for a nice profit," Dan explained. Where Matt squandered windfalls of cash on pot, beer, and partying, Dan was frugal and bristled when his younger brother referred to him as a coupon-clipping tightwad.

"Hold onto your green for now. I'll think about it."

A few weeks later, Stringbean sold Dan his first pound of marijuana. Within weeks, Dan was buying hits of speed by the hundreds. The drugs were supplied by a group shipping from Mexico, Tucson, and LA. Within a year, both Matt and Dan added cocaine to their stock, which compounded not only the risks but Dan's paranoia. Dan refused to sell to anyone but the same people. Sometimes if he knew someone for months, he added them to the "safe sell" list. Matt didn't harbor these same qualms. The hard drugs, as well as illegal steroids, were transported into Sioux Falls by having a runner hop on a plane with a one-way ticket to Los Angeles, connect with the supplier, and load up a suitcase with the goods. From LA, the drugs were brought back on a charter bus, thus avoiding airline security and the risk of being pulled over on the interstate in a car.

Chapter 18
If All You Have Is a Hammer, Everything Looks Like a Nail

Children learn what they live, but what the old adage doesn't tell you is where they live. Those raised in dysfunctional families within harsh neighborhoods more often than not end up raising their own dysfunctional families in a harsh neighborhood. It's as if an unseen metaphysical connection attracts kids with backgrounds like Matt's to be drawn to each other like shards of metal to a magnet. It was the dysfunctional skill set of cracking, distrust, and a back-alley knack for shooting pool and fist fighting that led Matt to Phil, a walking piece of dynamite packed with an unstable anger that came from years of being his dad's booze-fueled punching bag. The two of them met one evening in the haze of a smoke-filled billiards hall and quickly recognized that they shared a sharp eye and a hustler's-style savvy on a billiard's table that kept easy money flowing into their pockets. They began lifting weights together five times a week until Matt matured to 6' 1" and 215 pounds of violent aggression complete with a firecracker temper easily ignited by the smallest spark, coincidentally fitting of his entrance into the world on July 4th. He threw a right punch with devastating results. Phil, a former standout wrestler, and a stocky 200 pounds, was an overachiever with pent-up energy who, oddly enough, drank coffee in order to calm down. Putting these two tempers together was like mixing hydrogen sulfide and nitric acid; an explosive combination.

Over the next two years, they frequented the roughest joints in search of opponents with inflated views of their billiard skills. The yang of this easy money was unfortunately balanced by the yin of the countless fights that broke out during drunken games of pool when the final shot sunk the eight-ball into a pocket with a satisfying clink, and an inebriated opponent refused to pay his debt. Matt and Phil suffered broken hands and broken noses over the years, but in return, they put people in the hospital, and often they ended up there or in jail themselves. Matt's friends frequently referred to him as 21-21. He'd accumulated twenty-one arrests by the time he was twenty-one years old. Assaults, eluding, grand larceny, possession of stolen items, and DUIs resulted in a total of two years in the county jail but no time in the Big House. One reason he avoided prison was due to the skills of a good attorney paid with money earned from drug sales. On many occasions, Matt talked friends and associates into lying for him in police reports and in the courtroom. A few times he intimidated witnesses into not showing up for a preliminary hearing which generally resulted in the state's attorney dropping the charges. The drug business also helped pay the fines, but probation always hung over Matt's head. "The jail's a dump, has bad food, and no rec time," he mused. "It's probably better to be in prison," he said, not realizing his words were prophetic.

It started in a nightclub with an old, off-color prank; a favorite between two friends swathed in drunkenness and cockiness that had yet to be challenged to the breaking point. Phil waited for a girl to walk by Matt, and as she passed, Phil reached behind Matt and pinched her rear end before quickly pulling back and looking the other direction. This usually resulted in the girl yelling an obscenity or threat before storming off. This pretty brunette was different. Her eyes blazed with anger, and she got in Matt's face. "YOU'RE A JERK! DON'T EVEN THINK OF TOUCHING MY A** AGAIN!" she screamed, which caused a smirk to form at the corners of Matt's mouth. He knew he'd been set up. "YOU THINK IT'S FUNNY? WE'LL SEE HOW FUNNY IT IS WHEN I GET MY BOYFRIEND!" Matt drained his glass easily and motioned the waitress for another.

"Hold on!" Phil said, trying to block her path. "Look, we were horsing around, so don't go get your boyfriend or things will get real ugly, real fast." He tried reasoning with the girl, stopping short of an actual apology or admission of wrongdoing, but it was no use, and she disappeared into the dark, smoky club. Two minutes later she emerged, tailed by her boyfriend. The territorial dude didn't even have the chance to utter a threat before he found himself on the floor curled into the fetal position. Blood seeped from his twisted nose, forming a steadily growing pool of blood. Matt had hit him with a devastating knockout punch.

The girl tossed her hair back with a flick of her hand, tucked her head, and began pummeling Matt with both fists and screaming, "You'll pay for this, f***er!"

Matt pulled back his fist, unleashed a right hand that caught her square on the jaw, and sent her sprawling onto the floor, where she lay in a motionless heap alongside her boyfriend.

"The bitch wants to fight like a man, she can go down like one," Matt yelled. It was a harsh street code of conduct, the kind of thing polite society did not understand.

He pulled his hand to his chest. "Damn it, I broke my hand on her face, not on the guy!" It was true. Previous fractures had weakened his hand, which was now broken for the third time. To top it off, he was given a free ride to the county jail. When Dan bailed him out the next morning, Matt went to the emergency room and got another cast on his hand.

****

Weeks later, Matt pulled into the Pomp Room, a seedy bar already teaming with fuel-soaked patrons, but it was miles from the site of his last arrest. With a bourbon water in hand, he and Phil teamed up against two brothers for a game of pool.

"Losers buy the next round of drinks." Matt made the call, and the men nodded in agreement. The guys turned out to be skilled players, so the game turned intense, and Matt had no qualms about unethical pool shots. It was an unspoken rule to play by the gentleman's rules of etiquette, but Matt was no gentleman. A country song about drinking too much whiskey blared in the background, and Matt turned to Phil. "Dirty Daddy's gonna hafta play a little deviant pool," he said, draining his glass and swelling with bourbon bravery.

"Nah, don't get a fight started yet," Phil countered.

"Hell, yes. This is for drinkies."

Matt didn't have a good shot so instead tapped a pool ball, causing it to roll just far enough to ruin the next player's shot. It was legal, yet almost certain to cause trouble. The brothers turned to each other in unison. The taller one with a barrel belly sported a plaid shirt with overstretched buttons that puckered like a line of rectums. He shook his head, made the best shot he could, missed, then looked back at his brother while lightly shaking his head at the injustice of it all. His brother, stocky and sporting a broken nose that indicated he was no stranger to a fistfight, was slowly turning red-faced. When Matt's turn was up again, he made another dirty shot which he followed up with drunken taunting when the stocky brother took aim with his pool cue. "Don't miss now!" The words stumbled from Matt's thickening tongue when he leaned in over the table. The man swore, threw his cue on the table, and stepped toward Matt. It erupted into a four-man brawl.

In the movies, fights are portrayed unrealistically with a lot of punching, which does occur but not as the primary fighting technique. They don't show the eye gouging, biting, head-slamming, or dangerous head-kicking typical of a street or bar fight. Phil tackled the taller brother and then used the man's hair to bounce his head off the tile floor. Matt performed a near-perfect double-leg takedown on the broken-nosed brother, lifting the guy high off his feet before slamming him onto his back atop a bar table loaded with drinking glasses. The guy's back shattered most of the glasses, which took the fight right out of him.

The police radio squealed to life, and the officer held the receiver to his mouth. "I have a Matthew Lofton and Philip Hamman in custody and am en route to the county jail," he reported then listened to the static-laced reply. Matt kicked the back of the cop's seat, his calm expression never changing.

"F***er has nothing better to do on a Friday night than harass us." Matt scowled.

"You know how it is, bro. Last man standing goes to lockup," Phil reminded him. It was true. It didn't usually matter who started the fight but rather who was left upright to arrest.

"Think they'll press charges?" Phil asked.

"Probably," Matt said, kicking the back of the seat again.

The brothers didn't press charges. They knew that good things come to those who wait.

Chapter 19
The Mane Attraction

After his release from Plankinton a few years prior, Matt built a tangled network of illegal activities that often involved Dan. He moved from a hardened street thug into the calculating mastermind of any criminal opportunity that came his way.

"In this city, there is indeed a need for weed and speed," Dan bragged and suppressed a smile which indicated his pride in the corny phrase he spit out without even having to search for rhymes. He stirred the canned soup simmering on the stove top and then returned to the kitchen table, where he scooped marijuana into small baggies attached to a scale. Matt made no response and pulled on a T-shirt he plucked from the closet. He wasn't one to stick around the house or watch TV and planned on taking a ride on his cycle instead. "I'm making my mark on this city." Dan nodded toward the neat rows of baggies. "What the hell are you gonna do with your life?"

"I'm gonna learn how to cut hair. I've got the magic fingers, you know," Matt said, making an obscene gesture.

"Yeah, right," Dan scoffed.

"I'm serious. I walked past Stewart's on my way to work, and they have ads in the window for their hairstyling school. I have an appointment to sign up tomorrow."

"You're going to beauty school? Like a chick?"

"I'm gonna make me some honest cash."

Dan shifted position in the chair that had grown uncomfortable, removed his handgun from the waistband of his pants, and briefly brandished it in the air before placing it in his rear pocket. "Honest don't make you money. That's the problem."

Matt's primary reason for applying to the school, though, was that his desire for money and fast cars was matched only by his desire for the opposite sex. When he saw the ad for Stewart's School of Hairstyling, his first thought was that it would be a great place to meet girls. So he walked in and made an appointment to enroll right then and there. Mary was ecstatic that he'd turned a corner and decided to pursue an honest job in the same field for which she originally trained. The typically quiet Mary crowed about this transformation to her friends and already had some initial ideas for a graduation party.

The door of Stewart's School of Hairstyling opened to a modern, glam office of glass tables and funky avocado green chairs all overpowered by the pungent odor of perms and hairspray. Matt strode past a towering mirror and noticed stray hairs which he smoothed back and anchored with a dab of spit. The desk was sparse and orderly, which matched the appearance of the perfectly coiffed lady behind it. Her oversized glasses with their tinted lenses fit the hip image of the salon, and when she smiled, Matt wasn't surprised to see that she had orthodontically perfect teeth.

She explained in a tinkling voice that the school had immediate scholarships available, and Matt warmed inside at this unexpected gold nugget.

"The money is allotted every two months as long as you're enrolled and can be used for food, living expenses, and tuition. Would you be interested in applying?"

"Oh, definitely," Matt said, already scheming to find out how to use the money for partying expenses while ensuring he'd never pay it back. The real opportunity here, the one Matt didn't see, was the chance to find a wholesome girl with the drive to make something of herself. He thought just far enough ahead to consider the windfall of booze and pot this loan would bring yet not far enough to consider what would happen when he never repaid it. *It's school,* he reasoned. *They'll wait until I've graduated, then good luck collecting.* It was a scam that wouldn't quite work out the way he hoped. In fact, quite a few things at Stewart's would have unexpected consequences.

The students learned everything they needed to know in the first ninety days of instruction. In typical Matt style, he cut classes, didn't read the assignments, but still managed to perform adequately when his class started on the floor styling customers who were willing to get a novice perm, haircut, or dye job for a reduced price. It burned Matt that someone else had what he considered a good scam going.

"Stewart's has a sweet deal here. They rake in money from us paying to go to school, and then they rake it in from the customers on top of it," he mentioned to a girl from his class during a break in a cramped room crowded with cheap tables and plastic chairs. "We work hard, too. On our feet all day." He reached for the newspaper and turned to the classifieds to search for a cheap car or motorcycle to fix up and resell for a small profit.

The girl inched her chair toward Matt and tilted her head in a dramatically sensual manner. "Yeah, but my motto is 'Work hard, play hard,' and I do know how to play hard."

Matt folded the paper and tossed it aside. "I know how to play, too, baby."

"If you're not doing anything, come to a party at my house tonight," she offered.

"Yeah, I could probably stop by," Matt said casually. He worked his charm on these girls as easily as any other scam. Few of them were as street-wise as Matt, and many were in the market for a handsome bad boy with his all-knowing ways. Business was good.

"Bring some friends, if you want, and uh, actually we were wondering if you could buy us some beer."

Most of the girls there were eighteen years old. Matt was twenty-one, good-looking, and his reputation as a willing purveyor of alcohol slithered through the female grapevine. He latched onto this unexpected opportunity to make a few bucks two or three times a week by buying a case of Steinhaus beer for $4.62 and reselling it for ten bucks to the underage crowd of girls fresh out of high school. Though the girls unknowingly paid him double the price for the beer, they were fully willing to give him what he wanted in the bedroom. The downside to this was that his nocturnal prowling brought out the cat in some of the girls. He wasn't a swooning man who fell in love with doe-eyed innocent girls nor steel-nerved bad girls. Much like a tomcat, a relationship was out of the question. Friction around the school culminated with words like *slut* and *whore* being thrown around the break room, and an occasional student stylist storming out of the school in tears.

Not all the future hairstylists realized he came from the rough. Matt was deceptive in hiding most of his dirty deeds, and one girl in particular found herself attracted to this confident charmer. Something drew Matt to her repeatedly, and they spent many evenings together, yet he was still incapable of commitment or love despite her many promising qualities. When she found herself pregnant, Matt was no longer interested, so she packed up and went back home to Minnesota, where she gave birth to a baby girl.

The cat fights escalated. Matt was only there for the girls, and it became apparent that a half-hearted effort at work was no longer enough. When it was his turn to apply hair color the next day, he just didn't show up, knowing he wasn't prepared. To top it off, he hadn't made a single payment on his loans, and the school was asking questions. He never returned again.

"I already spent the money," he said with a shrug to Dan before tossing away a letter that arrived from the school's attorney demanding payment. The next week another letter arrived threatening to sue and garnish his wages if necessary. Since he'd recently been arrested and spent the weekend in jail, he decided to start making payments.

"Damn. Those f***ers are rich, and they still want more money," he lamented while writing out a check and contemplating all the repercussions of having ever seen the ad for Stewart's School of Hairstyling.

Chapter 20
The Wild West

A blurred fluorescent light quivered into focus, and the room tilted. A wave of nausea sloshed through Matt's stomach. He blinked at the light, then moaned and curled up to ease the crushing pain that throbbed within his ribcage. It brought to his mind that cliché about feeling as though he'd been run over by a truck. He blinked into the light and went to reach for the IV in his forearm but found his wrist was handcuffed to the bed frame. Then the memories oozed back, and he recalled the explosive blast of a firearm and then blackness.

Ten hours prior, rock music pulsed from the wall-to-wall speakers into the weed-covered front lawn of a weathered house in a ramshackle neighborhood dotted with homes well-versed in the art of a good weekend kegger; something that always sounded like a good idea but rarely was. Matt's gift for turning an ordinary night into something memorable meant he had a collection of loyal but rowdy friends who gravitated in his orbit of parties and good times. On this night, he and three buddies, Phil, MB, and Wilbur, reeled from the car, each carrying a drink, with Wilbur still complaining to Matt, "You got piles of weed, and you didn't bring me one joint, Cheap Charlie."

"No dough, no go," Matt replied.

They passed a sea of girls with feathered hair and skin-baring tops, and a few of them loudly and shamelessly flirted with a hopeful group of teenage boys wearing cowboy hats and blue jeans, despite the summer heat. The girls' loud talk melted into giggles when MB let out a wolf whistle, and Matt made some brazen comments about their womanly physical attributes. They responded with a seductive challenge about how *we're too much for you guys to handle*, yet surveyed the four skeptically as they passed by. The crash pad of a house was now standing room only, and with over a hundred half-sloshed partiers, some spilled into the yard and the neighboring lawns. Wilbur gave a head nod and a ready smile to several people he recognized. As he pushed through the crowd, people shouted to hear themselves above the blaring music. With his upbeat personality, he was the first of the group to laugh and keep things lighthearted but turned violent if anyone threatened a friend. He leaned over an end table, poured the fifth of whiskey he'd brought with him into plastic glasses, and handed one to Matt.

Sensing a threat, Matt did a quick 180 upon hearing a broody voice behind him.

"Why'd you start crap at the bar the other night when you were the one cheating?" It was the taller billiards player from the Pomp Room brawl. At his side was the stocky brother, his chest puffed out, along with their third brother and two additional friends who stood with their arms folded over their chests. Matt didn't cower at this obvious attempt to pull off the intimidation act. Instead, his face erupted into a ball of red. When Matt's blood was whiskey-dampened, he jumped at the chance for a fight. He curled his fist and unleashed a devastating right hand into the guy's face which sent him flying back into the crowd of partiers. The mostly drunken horde pushed the guy right back to Matt, and a few people yelled, "Take it outside!" So they did.

Like a scene from the Wild West, the two groups started punching and whirling tornado-style across the lawn. Matt scuffled into the street and grappled the taller brother to the ground and then pummeled him with an elbow to the face, saying, "Now how tough are you, Big Bird?" And when the exertion and alcohol made his head go light, Matt stood up, and Big Bird broke away. Matt walked over to take a turn on Shortcake, as he called the stocky brother, claiming that if he got hit too hard, his cream filling would spill out. The fighting mushroomed into chaotic violence, and the brawlers switched from punching and stomping one foe to attacking another. Wilbur turned around and caught sight of Big Bird half a block down the road with something in his hand.

"DON'T DO IT!" someone from the crowd shouted, and heads snapped in that direction. The belated warning acted like a switch that made the scene fade into slow motion. Big Bird had run to his vehicle and now reappeared from the haze of darkness holding a shotgun. The slide of a 12-gauge being pumped silenced the rumbling crowd of onlookers just as an explosion echoed through the neighborhood. Wilbur staggered backward clutching his leg and screams rocketed through the air along with cries to call the cops. People scattered like cockroaches. Just when Big Bird perched the gun back on his shoulder, MB sprang from behind, superhero-style, and grappled Big Bird. Wilbur, though wounded, joined in. They proceeded to stomp and kick the trigger man's head on the street with his skull making a sound like a bowling ball thudding onto the pavement. The guy turned over in resignation, but MB just stood up and started kicking him in the face again until someone yelled, "I think he killed that dude!" Undeterred, Wilbur then grabbed the shotgun and slammed it repeatedly on the street, grunting and swearing, until the weapon lay shattered. One of the most vicious fighters of the group, Wilbur didn't stop until he was certain no one would use that gun on his friends again.

Even after the loud roar of the shotgun blared across the fight scene, Matt cursed as he clambered to his feet in the middle of the road then swung wildly at Shortcake, each trying to gain control of the other. Seeing that the fight had escalated out of control and desperate to get away, the third brother made a rash decision and jumped into his pickup to escape. He squealed away from the curb and, without realizing it, bounced over Matt and his own brother, sending the two skidding along beneath the vehicle until they eventually came flopping and flipping out from behind as the pickup barreled away into the darkness. The two lay unconscious, their bloody bodies twisted and contorted on the cold cement. Sirens blared in the distance, and soon two sheriff cars, a highway patrol, and two ambulances filled the street. The swirling lights attracted the neighborhood looky-loos like a bug light.

Matt woke up in the hospital to find he had severe internal injuries, broken ribs, and a dislocated hip. The skin was scraped off his arms and legs where he had been dragged beneath the pickup. Wilbur was down the hall shot up on morphine after having buckshot removed from his legs, hips, and stomach. Big Bird was in a coma overnight. Several warrants were issued, but Matt sidestepped charges with a self-defense plea and a good lawyer courtesy of drug money from Dan. He escaped death once again, all of it due to a drunken argument over a billiard game for drinks.

Chapter 21
Luck Happens

Matt was a player. Not that he kept score or even bragged about his female conquests, whom he forgot about again the next morning and vice versa for the most part. He had no desire to tie himself down to someone else's whims. Besides, he was a wanderer. Dan was not. He'd been dating a girl for over a year, and when she gave birth on a bitterly cold January day, Dan was overcome with the feeling that there was something extraordinary about this howling baby boy who'd burst forth at the start of a new year that marked the nation's bicentennial. His intuition puzzled his small family since none of their relatives had ever amounted to anything with bragging rights. The little baby, Wade, gave Dan something to brag about. But Dan was away. He'd made an attempt to clean up his life and was in the military. Ultimately, this structured life didn't appeal to him. He was soon back to the civilian life and back to his old ways. Wade remained with his mom and only had occasional contact with Dan for the first few years.

A bundle of money lay just beyond a bong-induced haze for any gutsy person willing to take a chance in the local drug trade. Dan was business-minded. Matt was devious, though he sometimes planned schemes with meticulous detail and at other times seized an opportunity to which he gave no thought. Together they built a lucrative drug trade, intending to only sell marijuana until the financial lure of cocaine made them a main supplier of illegal party drugs in the Sioux Falls area. Being intimately familiar with the regulars in lockup and running in the fast lane, the duo had no shortage of corrupt friends, which meant they never lacked for customers.

For years, the system ticked along smoothly. Matt found his forte, but good was never good enough. There was that internal pull, as strong as the need to breathe, that left him always wanting more, better, or different. Whatever he did, he did to the best of his ability. His successes left him feeling invincible. What they lacked at times was a supplier. Word on the street was the other small-time dealers turned white at the thought of muling their own drugs in from hot spots in California or Arizona. There were horror stories circulating of dealers left rotting in some border town jails, which meant that most local suppliers were content to buy a few pounds rather than cart in their own truckload. So when others got cold feet and backed out, Matt remained unshakably in the game and saw an opportunity to move up the rungs of this Midwestern drug trade as a challenge. His ace was nerves of steel that emitted self-confidence in a way that washed him of suspicion and allowed him to avoid the police radar. In the drug trade, he remained lucky, although he was arrested for other charges. Anytime Matt drank, he grew bourbon-bold and started itching for a fight, so assault and battery led the arrest list.

"That's why they're small time, and I'll have a bulging bank balance." Matt crumpled another parking ticket and tossed it in the garbage.

Dan threw his brother a challenging look. "I'm the one with the green. Anytime you start to pile up cash, you blow it on a motorcycle or car."

"Yeah, I don't got no moths flying out of my wallet like you, and you can't take it with you in the end." Matt felt no jealousy of Dan's success or wealth, preferring to spend his money while he had the chance.

He had never intended to transport drugs, but as an opportunist, he had little willpower to refuse a deal that promised a quick buck. A drug-dealing associate who was too skittish to mule the goods himself eventually led Matt to connections in Tucson, and the business flourished. Years of learning from his mistakes helped Matt develop a sixth sense for avoiding detection. By now, he could almost divine the DEA's pattern of checkpoints. He quickly realized that his Tucson contacts had the same way of thinking that he did, and this small group watched out for each other with zeal. They knew that if one of them went down, they'd likely all go down as one person turned on the next in return for reduced charges. They relied on each other to find which roads weren't currently set up with drug stops, so the word went out as to which highways were generally safe to travel with a trunkload of drugs. Matt was cautious and methodical, never failing to scout out a road in advance and knowing that this extra precaution was the reason he didn't get caught. The only way it could fail was if, by some bizarre stroke of bad luck, the police set up a stop in the small window period between Matt or his cohorts checking the road and the time when he left with his shipment.

For months this seemingly airtight system worked for all of them. Matt grew bolder and more confident with each successful run.

"You don't got the stomach for this," he challenged Dan, who had claimed the trip was too long for his van that needed some motor work. "That's why I'm the one who does the tough jobs."

And he was disciplined in muling drugs, never careless. Yet one day he went sailing down an Arizona highway which was supposed to be clean, the noon sun covering the canyon in a spotlight of white heat. When he came over the crest of a hill, he slowed upon seeing that traffic had snarled into a stretch of cars snaking forward at a drug stop, and he swore furiously. Flashing lights twirled up ahead, and the police had placed a long, metal swinging gate across the two-lane highway to prevent anyone from trying to floor it and outrun the cops. One agent with an automatic weapon scanned the line of cars for suspicious behavior while two others, led by a drug dog, walked around a stopped car. Matt counted twenty vehicles that stood between him and the agents. Even though the air conditioning was running full blast, sweat beaded on his upper lip. The waves of heat pulsating outside the window rendered him nauseous. Rather than panicking, he sorted through his options before realizing there were none. Turning around would be a guarantee to send the police roaring after him. Matt drummed his fingers and let out a slow breath. For some reason, the DEA agents seemed to be taking an extraordinary amount of time with the sports car now at the front of the line. Their dog stopped, then proceeded. One of the guards mouthed something to the dog that Matt couldn't discern from this distance. The dog continued sniffing around the car for the second time. Then just like that, they pulled the dog back, and one officer escorted the driver back to the squad car. Matt swore loudly. With all the crime going on in the big cities around here, these petty DEA maggots had nothing better to do than slow the flow of traffic, he reasoned. A wad of bile rose in his throat which he could barely swallow. He hadn't faced a situation like this in years, and the memories of too many jail cells came flooding back. Just when he considered flooring the car in the other direction and risking the dismal odds of getting away, the line of cars started rolling ahead, and the shifting angle of the metal cars under sun sent glints of light spraying here and there across the desert. Matt shook away the jitters. Other punks might crumble under this pressure, but that's why he was here, and they weren't. The blood drained from his head, and as the line of cars again slowed to a stop, he shifted into park and realized his hands were unsteady. A ringing sound within his brain sickened him again. In the frozen moment, a film of cold sweat glazed his back.

Traffic was backed up nearly to the hill now, so the agents couldn't stop everyone. The driver of the sports car returned to his vehicle, and they waved him through along with a few cars before stopping a tow truck. It was a random inspection site. Matt was only three cars away and worried the dog would smell the load of drugs from this distance. He fought back an overwhelming urge to vomit and instead breathed slowly to ease the pounding in his chest. The DEA finished with the tow truck and waved it through along with the next six cars, including Matt's. He had to move by slowly, 10 to 15 mph, nodding politely at the officers who gave him long looks as he passed. He didn't bask long in this lucky break.

The system needed a tweak, so Matt devised a two-car runner system, which meant he started bringing an associate, someone with no prior felonies, who was willing to drive for a nice cash payment and free drugs once they got back to Sioux Falls. With that incentive, he had no trouble finding a mule. If Matt got arrested with a load of drugs, it could be life in prison as a habitual criminal. Instead, the associate would mule the drugs in one car with Matt following behind. That way he could keep an eye on his investment but stay safely a few car lengths behind. Once the drugs got to Sioux Falls, he pulled back and only sold to trusted customers. For a while.

"One meek little coward who gets his stupid ass pinched by the cops is all it takes to bring me down," he'd heard from one of the suppliers years ago, and it stuck with him.

Chapter 22
Clientele

The front porch of this rental house on the stockyards side of town swayed beneath the weight of its aged boards. The shades were pulled which cast the inside with perpetual gloom, but that was a typical feeling around this place. Someone was passed out on the couch while a team of flies buzzed around a heap of empty beer cans sitting on a low coffee table. The current occupant of the home was a part-time tattoo artist and former jail time acquaintance of Matt's. He popped in and out of the county jail periodically to serve short sentences for misdemeanors such as simple assault or resisting arrest; charges that had been pled down from more serious offenses.

"This is the cheapest security guard you can buy. One hundred bucks." The gun runner placed the AK-47 in Matt's hands and motioned for him to give it a try. "Comes with a twenty-round clip."

Matt pulled back the bolt and felt a surge of power sighting down the barrel. The surges never lasted long enough. "I like this bad boy," and he tossed a Benjamin onto the table knowing his brother would be pleased. Dan loved weapons, and they needed something to protect the thousands of dollars in cash and illegal drugs hidden beneath floorboards in his bedroom closet. Dan owned an assortment of assault rifles, shotguns, and handguns. "Let someone try to rob us now, and I'll feed 'em a nice bite of a .357," Dan quipped to Matt.

When you run a drug house, the clientele ranges from pathetic to disgusting. There were the hophead girls skittering around like fleas until dawn hoping for a free white line and eventually doing anything to get it, scumbag lowlifes who'd never worked an honest day, and convicts with shady pasts and sneaky hands. One regular was a guy nicknamed Top Hat, a scuzzy hillbilly with long, greasy hair and a teardrop tattoo below his eye.

Matt was boozy from bourbon, and as usual, that brought out the hatred that fermented just below his surface. Even on a good day, there was a meanness about him that tainted every action, and the alcohol merely inflated this. For no good reason, he stepped a toe's length from Top Hat. "Listen, you dirtball; I don't like your crusty a** hanging around here day and night, so get the hell out of here." Top Hat looked at Matt and widened his eyes before taking an uneasy step back. He recognized the coldness that now clouded Matt's eyes and knew Matt's history of striking unprovoked, though he'd yet to be on the receiving end. Top Hat stood there not knowing what to do and flicking his tongue nervously between the gap where his two front teeth should have been. When Top Hat didn't move, Matt's temper flashed, and when that happened, he went off like a supernova. Top Hat was on the floor with Matt above him giving consecutive punches to the face; Top Hat quickly curled into a ball. Matt gave him one last right hand before walking away, then suddenly felt an odd sensation of warmth running down his leg.

"What the—?" Matt wiped at the crimson stain spreading across his blue jeans and down his pant leg before feeling the sharp pain in his hip. He glanced back at Top Hat, who was writhing on the ground moaning, then saw the bloody buck knife still clutched in his hand. Matt's face grew hot, and he sprinted toward Top Hat, kicking him repeatedly in the head until he'd worked himself into a sweaty frenzy to protests of, "Stop, brother! We ain't got no bad blood!" When the last of the anger slipped away, Top Hat was still. Matt washed the wound, wrapped it up, and fell into a drunken sleep. Matt never called the cops on Top Hat. He never called the cops on anyone. Ever. Two days later he went to the doctor. It was too late to get stitches, so he settled for a round of antibiotics. It was the last they saw of Top Hat.

Every job has its perks. The "good times" girls who flocked to Dan's house found out which men had money for drugs, and then circled them like vultures. These girls had built-in sensors and knew just when the house pulsed to life with a wild party. Thus began a procession of seedy girls in skin-baring tops with too-blonde hair, sunken eyes, and jacked up bangs. But with their presence, the monotonous days regularly erupted into parties where alcohol led to drugs and drugs led to sex. Every time.

A silver keg of beer flowed in the kitchen, and a crowd of people gathered around a coffee table in the living room sharing a bong. Over the blare of a stereo, laughter from a throng of partiers seeped into the bedroom where Matt spread some powder into a straight white line on the nightstand. He handed a rolled up bill to the blonde druggie and glanced down her unbuttoned blouse. He and Dan only occasionally indulged in cocaine, generally sticking to the business end of the drug trade. She hovered her nose above the tube for the briefest moment before inhaling deeply, then threw her head back and moaned, close-eyed. Matt responded with an impatient frown. She was just another shred of a woman who contained only the withered parts that remain after years of existing on nothing but coke, alcohol, and occasional junk food.

"Now, baby, we can get a private party going," he said.

Later, he nudged the girl, feeling mostly disgust at her spaced-out grin. The light in her eyes had died out years ago. He wanted her to leave for many reasons, not the least of which was that she'd likely rob him blind and later deny it if he dared fall asleep. She grunted but didn't move. "Debbie," he whispered. Her brows cinched together into a dart. "Dawn?" Her name definitely started with a *D*. Or was that the last girl? The names and faces blended together; they were nothing more than damaged goods, and each time he picked a new one from the swelling pile before tossing her back at the end of the night. All it cost was the price of a white line.

"*You've* never had a serious girlfriend," Dan commented, indicating this rendered him superior due to his ability to bond to another human.

"Beer. Pool. A girl. What's the difference? They all give you a bit of fun. No girl is worth more than a quick romp in the sack."

It was the same conversation he had with Mary. Settle down. Get an honest job. Start a family.

The aroma of fried chicken, cornbread, and beans hung in the air when Matt sat down to have supper with Mary. His dad was from the south, and even though they'd never shared this meal together—hell, the old man died when Matt was only eight—he had a baffling fondness for this southern food that tasted of happiness and nostalgia. Maybe it was something he inherited, but the meal filled him with satisfaction disproportionate to what one might expect from a piece of chicken, though he never mentioned it to Mary. Tonight he noticed the uncomfortable silence that preceded her soapbox lectures about settling down

"My greatest joy in life is you boys. You're missing out on what life is all about."

"If we're your greatest joy, you got cheated," Matt said, pouring syrup on the cornbread then licking the drips from his fingers. "I just wanna take care of myself and not have to worry about other people on top of it. What's wrong with enjoying life and doing what makes me happy?"

"Selfishness is the biggest curse on mankind, and it won't bring you happiness. I want you to be happy. Family is happiness."

"I'm not selfish. I'm hedonistic, and I like it that way. It works for me. Nice guys finish last. Conquer or be conquered." He'd spent a lifetime making emotional withdrawals from people and rarely making deposits.

"Well, I hope you don't get conquered by the law. You could end up in prison," Mary said just enough to let Matt know she realized what he was up to without lecturing.

The thing he couldn't explain to Mary was that he wouldn't get caught. Each time he tripped up, he learned a lesson, and now there was nothing left to learn. He was at the top of the game. He was Matt the Man again.

Chapter 23
Casualty

A party had been raging inside Dan's house for hours when he decided he needed to meet someone at Stockman's Bar, a narrow brick building on the rough edge just a step away from the railroad tracks. If the police were called to a late-night bar fight, odds were good they were headed to this place. The combination of drugs and alcohol sent Dan's body temperature into overdrive. He sat on his motorcycle guzzling cold beer, then kick-started the cycle and roared down the street, his head crouched down to catch the wind. As he soared down a side street, the wind puffed out his thin T-shirt, sending it flapping in the wind. He pushed the accelerator to 60 mph. The thrill of racing at top speed, cheating danger, and the purr of the gears filled him with an adrenaline rush nearly as satisfying as a line of coke. It was a thrill that made him feel invincible; he could do anything. Then ten blocks down, his cycle crashed into another vehicle at a crossroad. Brakes screeched, metal crunched, and the impact tossed him mercilessly through the air. Dan's body flipped and rolled along the cold cement street, and within minutes, the sound of the sirens grew steadily louder. Dan was oblivious to the dizzying array of emergency radios, static, flashing lights, and a growing crowd of onlookers. He'd landed thirty feet from his motorcycle, now a twist of metal.

"He's gotta be dead," several people in the crowd murmured.

The next morning Matt woke to a ringing phone. It might have rung earlier, but he slept through it. It was a friend calling. Dan had been in an accident last night, and this friend happened to live right where it occurred. Matt sat up quickly, and the blood rushed away from his face. Both drivers had been drinking, and though Dan had been speeding, the other car had turned into his lane.

Later he had foggy memories of getting dressed and somehow managing to meet Mary at the hospital, where a doctor cast his eyes downward before breaking the news that if Dan lived, he wouldn't walk again. When Mary heard the word *paraplegic*, she dissolved into a sobbing heap on a cold hospital chair, but not for long. In typical Mary fashion, she was soon filling out a mountain of forms, making phone calls, and visiting Dan during his months of rehab located hours away in Wisconsin at a veterans hospital. Fortunately for Dan, he'd served a stint in the army, and though the military discipline failed to settle him down, it did qualify him for extensive care.

After a few months of rehab, he returned home and went right back down the same wrong path. He resumed his drug operation and continued his life of crime from a wheelchair and a van custom-fitted with hand controls. For a day or so after he was first home, Matt treated him with kid gloves, but it just wasn't their way. The comfort came in knowing that no matter what one of them said or did, they were still brothers, and both of them tested this theory frequently.

"Give me twenty bucks, and I'll go buy us some dinner," Dan said in his typical tight-wad attempt to save a few bucks.

"F*** you, Shorty," Matt said, rummaging through cupboards and inspecting each glass until he found one without a chip in it and then helping himself to a tall glass of Jim Beam.

"I'm not short. I'm six-one."

"Not now. You're about four-foot-three."

116

No blow was considered too low between the brothers, and Matt was not about to let Dan lose his edge and get soft in what would now be an even harder world for him.

Matt (left) and Dan (right) during the height of their drug-dealing days

Dan, in his wheelchair, following a wild party that ended in paralysis.

Chapter 24
Welcome to the Big Time

Morning sun glared like a spotlight through the towering windows of the granite block courthouse onto the defendant's table. Matt stood facing the judge who was ready to announce his sentence and still hoping he might squeak by somehow. He hadn't slept well the night before. He'd fought against a twist of wire that had broken loose from the metal support beneath the emaciated mattress stained with the body fluids of past inmates housed in the county jail. It would take one of those acts of God Mary was always talking about, but he held onto that imaginary thread anyway.

He had built up a lucrative fencing ring for stolen goods. Petty thieves and druggies valued the confidential services he provided. When these convicts filched valuables from someone's house or car, it wasn't easy for them to turn the items into cash or drugs. They couldn't go to a pawn shop because these businesses received updated reports of stolen goods and were required to report any thieved items that crossed their desk. Most of these crooks didn't have friends or relatives with extra money, or they'd stolen the item from a friend or relative in the first place. With the right connections and enough desperation, their path would eventually lead them to Matt's front door. For a hefty commission, Matt would take the $800 ring they lifted from grandma's jewelry box and hand them $50 in cash or cocaine. Matt developed a powerful rhythm for unloading the items. Eventually, he would take them to a pawn shop several hundred miles away. Sometimes he found a shady buyer within his circle of cohorts as he did with Burl, an old friend who understood that once you bought a fenced good, it stayed bought.

Matt acquired a load of items from a burglary and sold a diamond ring to this friend who wanted to give it to a girl. When Burl found himself strapped for cash, he broke the unwritten code of conduct and brought it to a nearby pawn shop, where it was identified as stolen. Within hours Burl pointed to Matt as the supplier in exchange for a lighter sentence. Now, on this chilly day in 1982, twenty-two-year-old Matt faced this charge and one for aggravated assault, a felony in which Matt sent a man to the hospital with broken bones after a vicious bar fight. When the judge returned from reviewing the lawyers' arguments, the few members of the courtroom rose.

"You are sentenced to a term of ten months in the state penitentiary." The judge smacked his gavel, and the tenuous thread he was holding finally snapped. There was no act of God that day. Before the echo of the gavel on wood stopped reverberating, his illusion of invincibility disappeared along with his freedom. His insides suddenly liquefied. He wanted to sit, faint maybe, but someone ushered him out of the room and into the closest thing he had to a phobia, the unknown. Although he'd made countless trips to jail, this was different. "The house on the hill" was how inmates referred to it in jail, but those words no longer slipped so easily from his tongue now that he was the one headed to the pen. Regret at straying from his criteria competed with the fury that came from imagining the payback he'd someday give Burl. One slip-up and suddenly he was the one paying the price for this meek little coward's move that fingered Matt. The word *snitch* bounced around inside Matt's head. These rats chirping to the man were his constant nemesis, and he had a nagging feeling it wouldn't end here.

A jailer shackled his hands and feet together and ushered him into the back of a deputy sheriff's car for the short trip to the penitentiary, an ancient stone beast built in 1881. Neither man spoke. Matt wasn't sure he could have said anything. His mouth had drained itself of saliva. His head went light, and he thought he might pass out or throw up, so he focused on his Mustang instead. Mary had that in the garage until he got out, but his mind kept spinning toward this foreign destination. He'd passed the South Dakota State Prison countless times. It stood on a hill overlooking Sioux Falls and had acquired the usual names for a building that served its purpose: The Big House, Graybar Hotel, Hard Rock Hotel. At the hill's base stood the meatpacking plant and sprawling stockyards that melted into neighborhoods and a bustling downtown. The van was already through a security gate and into the courtyard of the intake center. The place looked different today, a terrifying granite demon lording over the city with soaring block walls and steel-barred doors coiffed with spirals of concertina wire.

"Put the new fish over there." The pot-bellied jailer carted Matt there with nary a word, instead bobbing his head to the country music songs from the car radio of which Matt was scarcely aware. Even now the man gave the prison guard a quick nod and started writing something on a clipboard he picked up at the door but gave no acknowledgment to Matt, still in his orange jail jumpsuit, who'd just made the transition from being a person to becoming a meaningless number sentenced to so many months of being banished from society. He had not yet learned that this was a world outside the real world; a place that was gloomy and barbed. A place where you ceased to matter, friends forgot you, and family meant to visit, but *you know how time flies*. With a wave of the hand, while joking with the jailer about a ball game on TV, the guard ushered Matt to a small cell, and his previous life took its last breath.

His first cell was in the fish tank, a depressingly pale green block of cells where all first-timers stayed during several days of orientation. He sat on a hard folding chair for hours while a correctional officer or social worker explained the regulations and consequences for violations. The dress code was blue jeans and a white T-shirt. Matt could supply his own, or the clothing would be issued to him. The prison-supplied jeans were stiff and cheap though. The social worker spent an inordinate amount of time detailing educational options such as auto body classes, welding, and obtaining a GED. Matt preferred his time with the correctional officer who broke the boredom by punctuating the rules with a healthy dose of enthusiasm, inappropriate as it was. He listened intently, silently inspecting each rule for a loophole, but it wasn't until he was integrated with the general population that he realized the most important rules were the unwritten ones. The inmates who had served years of hard time were the creators and enforcers of the real code of conduct. Consequences were delivered swiftly and without empathy. Not learning these regulations could mean the difference between life and death, or at least harm.

The warden assigned him to West Hall, a section of the prison reserved for younger inmates and less violent offenders. The philosophy was to keep this group away from more hardened, institutionalized cons as much as possible. It worked for some. For Matt, prison time was the incubator for his hatred toward society; his animosity toward others, especially cops and snitches; and a distrust of "the system." Most cons shared the same defects. Volcanic tempers and the tendency to act first, think later. What they didn't have in common with Matt was his intellect or flagrant boldness. Yet Matt didn't just have a run-of-the-mill anger problem. When his temper blazed, the world went black, and he spent most of his waking hours teetering on the edge of explosive hatred and fury. Perhaps he was a carefree child during his time with Jack and Judy, but those feelings of contentment had dimmed to an old memory. The only feelings left were of contempt for the world.

The cell contained a cot, a toilet, and a sink. Every cell block was painted the colors of depression: gray, pale green, and dingy brown as if to foreshadow the ugliness in store for its troubled occupants. Three days into his sentence, Matt tripped over an unwritten rule. The day started out with no problems. He'd risen to the sound of the wake-up bell and dressed quickly. At 6:30, the cell door opened electronically, and he'd quickly gotten out on the tier knowing the door would close in six minutes. Anyone still inside their cell would have to go without breakfast. He was standing in line when a tap on his shoulder caught his attention.

"Hey, Fish, step back and let me in front of you." Matt turned to find a goofy-looking con with a receding hairline giving his best attempt at a threatening glare.

"If you want problems, you just found the right guy," Matt said in a serious tone, narrowing his eyes to a slit.

The con stepped nose-to-nose with Matt. "Listen, punk, you might wanna learn the rules—"

His words were cut short when Matt's right fist caught him square on the jaw, sending Goofy sailing to the floor. Two guards swooped in and led Matt away for his first write-up violation and a talk with the lieutenant on duty. Surprisingly, he got off easy with only a warning rather than a trip to "the hole" for a session of isolation and loss of privileges. But the prison operated like the wild, and inmates formed their packs. Now Matt had a worry. There was the possibility that this con had friends who might come back and retaliate.

Chapter 25
Unwritten Rules

Gradually Matt learned the rules of maximum security prison. *The sharks never sleep, and they're always looking to prey upon the small or weak. Protection is vital, but it's not cheap.* One of the few choices for a small, physically weak convict was to sell himself as a punk, a sexual toy, to a tougher con, an older inmate who happened to have a preference for a boy toy. Matt avoided the punks who adapted their looks to imitate a more feminine appearance.

In prison, you don't stare. Matt and his weight-lifting partner, Earl, were finishing a workout. The two had enough in common to form a prison-level friendship; they both liked the Steelers and lifting weights. Earl was a farm kid from South Dakota, big and built, with a large head, Frankenstein haircut, and squatter's butt that reminded Matt of a cartoon dinosaur named Earl, hence the nickname. Earl was married once and then found a girlfriend on the side who happened to work for the DEA. When he didn't leave his wife, the girlfriend accused him of rape, and of course, the court believed her story.

"Yeah, a jury screws you, and everyone says they did their civic responsibility, but you screw someone who changes her mind, and suddenly you're in here," Matt sympathized while spotting Earl on a 350-pound bench.

In prison, you don't ask questions. You figure it out. In the coming weeks, Matt noticed more powder women with their lips and underwear stained red from cherry juice or craft paint. These powder women wore their prison jeans low in the back, exposing the homemade pink panties. They looked vulnerable, but with a few well-placed complaints they had the power to create a storm of violence or bring down the steeliest con.

Matt was curling some dumbbells, noting that one of the only benefits of prison was plenty of time to work on his build. He awoke with nothing to do each day but dodge the endless manipulation and attempts to exploit. You had to be tough or become prey, so he lifted with the dedication of an Olympian. Earl finished a set of bench presses and sat up to take a quick break before the next set when Bobby Boy walked over, hands on hips.

"Hey, I want to use that bench press," he said, with lips pursed in a challenge to Earl.

Bobby Boy's daddy was Lurch, a hulking habitual criminal with a big head, bigger hands, and the biggest temper on the cell block. He wore his convictions of armed robbery, kidnapping, and aggravated assault like dysfunctional medals that had earned him a life sentence. These were status crimes; crimes along with killing cops and robbing banks that garnered respect among the inmates. Bobby Boy could move through the prison demanding privileges like the bench press even if he didn't really want it. Earl and Matt stepped back without a word.

In spite of their ability to irritate, when the powder women bickered, it provided a welcome break from the daily boredom.

"Stay away from my man, bitch!"

"You better start takin' care of your daddy, or I will!"

Matt wondered if anyone else, out of pure boredom, hoped the smack talk would escalate into a full-blown cat fight just for a few minutes of free entertainment. The powder women quarreled and bared their claws, wiggled when they walked and offered sexual favors in exchange for just about anything of great value.

Because of his size and his background as a fighter, Matt protected himself without the help of a prison daddy. He had no desire to get mixed up in boy toy problems. Getting through each day demanded constant vigilance. The Big House was teeming with career convicts and sociopaths who couldn't walk across a room without rustling up some problem or danger. Anyone who didn't know how to crack learned quickly, even though almost everyone on the inside had grown up with daily doses of cut-downs. It became habit to immediately notice physical imperfections in others to use at a later date to crack on the person. Hours of restless free time along with active minds were catalysts for corruption. The criminal mind sparkled with creativity when it came to producing a weapon out of the most unsuspecting item. A piece of wire from the welding shop could be crafted into a shank, a sharpened toothbrush or chicken bone ground into a sharp point, a shard of chrome smuggled from the auto body area quickly materialized into a knifepoint. Even newspaper could be tightly rolled to a needle-sharp point then solidified nearly to stone by lightly dripping hard water onto the paper over time.

Matt and Earl sat down with plastic trays containing toast and cereal. Matt set his fork to the side. He wouldn't need it but was given and was expected to return a spoon, fork, and butter knife after each meal or get written up. That reduced the potential for a piece of silverware to be stolen and used as a weapon. The din of a hundred men eating breakfast had become an almost soothing sound due to the predictability of this morning routine. Stability comforted Matt. On the inside, routines were predictable but were tempered by the underlying current of potential problems between inmates that could escalate in seconds. The possibility of a fight hung ever present in their midst, and no one could be trusted. The person who was your friend one week might rat you out the next using a secret you let slip.

"See the blond dude at the end of the far table?" Earl nodded his head to the right.

Matt ate a few bites of toast, waiting the appropriate amount of time before glancing at the far table.

"I call him Scam Man," Earl said. "Him and his cellmate got busted on a setup. We saw a big commotion on tier two, and I ran up to catch the action like a lot of people. A guard came elbowing through, and then the goon went skating across the bloody tier like he was on a Slip 'N Slide. Scam Man's cellmate was laying there unconscious with a ten-inch shank buried through his kidney." Earl scooped some jam on his toast, taking a few big bites before continuing the story with a semi-full mouth. "The guy lived, but it turned out the stabbing was a big setup. He wanted to get shipped out of this prison to some other state where he thought the parole board would be more lenient. Turns out, the dude had his own cellmate stab him but didn't think he'd be that brutal!"

"How'd they get caught?" Matt knew this was prison schooling at its finest. The ability to learn from others' mistakes was a vital skill.

"Some rat went singing to the warden and told him what happened. Scam Man and his cellmate got more convictions added to their sentence and more time."

"Who was the snitch?"

"Some scrawny punk who got his time cut short and is living it up out on the streets while we're stuck here. Them snitches never miss a chance to roll over on someone. They'll take you down faster than anyone else in here."

A loud buzz indicated it was time to return to their cells. Matt would read, watch television, or listen to the radio until 12:30, when the whole meal routine started again followed by an hour of rec time to lift weights or hang out. Another bell indicated the end of rec time, and then they passed the endless minutes until supper at 6:30. At 9 PM a bell preceded the doors opening for forty-five minutes of open tier time. Interspersed throughout all of this were four full prison counts at 9 AM, 2:30 PM, 7:30 PM, and 10 PM, 365 days a year. The numbers on each tier had to match the number of prisoners. No exceptions. Every prisoner had to "show skin." If someone was covered up and sleeping, he was woken up to show skin. The whole day was dictated by a series of shrill bells.

Chapter 26
The Bell Curve

Matt had all but forgotten about the tests the prison psych had given him upon his arrival.

"You have a meeting with the warden." A guard came to the cell, and Matt held an enviable poker face in spite of the sudden flutter in his chest. He clapped his *True West* paperback together, not thinking to bookmark the page. He didn't ask the guard the reason for the meeting since the guy would just say he didn't know, but Matt contemplated potential alibis on the way to the office.

The guard led him to a frugal office adorned with little more than a gold nameplate on the desk and file cabinets. There was no noise in the office, only the distant shouts of workmen somewhere down the hall. Matt was sure that if the room could talk, it would have warned him that this was not a good place to be summoned. He sat with his hands cuffed in front until the warden rushed in twenty minutes later offering no apologies. Warden Herman Solem was known for his belief in prison reform based on the philosophy of empowering inmates with decision-making and the ability to leave prison not just reformed but ready to lead productive lives.

He briefly made eye contact then flipped through a couple of folders before scrunching his eyes together. "Matthew Lofton." It wasn't a question, so Matt remained silent.

"I was reviewing the psychologist's report," he said, reaching behind him for the chair and sitting down, "when I came across

129

your IQ results." He looked up, but his eyes revealed nothing. "Have you had an IQ test before this one?"

"No, not that I remember," Matt said, reflexively giving a non-definite response that gave him an out should he need it for some reason.

The warden ran his finger down the paper once more, silently mouthing the words he was perusing before replacing the paper in its folder and once again locking eyes with Matt as though ready to interrogate him.

"According to your results, you have an IQ of 132. I imagine you know what that means."

Matt shrugged. "Not really, I guess."

The warden explained something about standard deviations and eventually concluded by saying, "You have what is considered *very superior intelligence*. In fact, anything over 140 is considered genius." He drummed two fingers on the table, waiting for Matt's reply.

Matt's poker face crumbled. He'd never heard that before, and this supposed compliment left him feeling both uncomfortable and bewildered.

"You have more potential academically than most people who will ever set foot in here. I will give you recommendations for any college or technical school you want to attend upon your release."

Matt listened patiently to the rest of the speech, nodding politely. At some point during the conversation, the idea of becoming an engineer or architect flickered in his mind. Math came to him naturally, and he had a flair for design. As a kid, he'd doodled endless sketches of buildings instead of working on assignments in school. He had an even greater talent for absorbing lessons from the street though. In the end, the predictability of an honest job simply couldn't compete with the thrill of a good scam.

"Yeah, I'll let you know," he said when the warden finally finished. He already knew though. He'd continue his career as a criminal and make sure he was more careful next time.

Once he got out, he was more careful. For a while. He called Phil to help him drum up a resume, and the final product indicated that Matt had spent the last year attempting to start up his own business. He used this to land a job with a welding company and soon picked up where he left off with the drug trade as well. This side business flourished, and one day he just didn't show up for his day job again.

One Christmas, Wade woke up smiling, knowing there was a present waiting for him. He was living with Dan, who had made some effort to decorate the house and even put up a tree that he wrapped with colorful lights. Wade bounced into the living room and then immediately took a few steps back and let out a little yell. Below the tree lay one of Dan's friends, bloody and still. Nearby lay another friend with a torn sweater and knuckles caked with dried blood. Wade's stomach knotted. He crept into the kitchen, worried about what else he might find when he decided to follow the suspicious spatters on the floor which led him out the door, where he found long smears of blood covering the porch and wheelchair ramp. He discovered his dad passed out in the bedroom, breathed a sigh of relief, and poured some dry cereal into a bowl.

The day stretched into afternoon with Wade expecting Christmas to start any minute.

He perked up when Mary arrived to cook a meal. "It's okay," he shouted to her over the blare of a sitcom he'd turned up hoping it would wake his dad. "They're not dead. They're just passed out!"

But Mary threw her arms up in defeat and shook her head, "I'm not cooking for this bunch of misfits!" She stormed around to go back home but turned to remind Wade, "Let your dad know I'm not too happy about this!"

With that, Wade's last bit of hope bled away, and he went to a friend's house.

By sixth grade, Wade was living with Dan full time while Matt was in prison. This house of drugs and corruption was a toxic atmosphere for Wade. Many mornings he opened his bedroom door and had to step over at least a half-dozen people who were passed out on the floor in various states of undress. In this unprincipled environment, he learned survival skills and how to fend for himself. In the evenings he watched side-eyed from the living room while Dan did triple beams of marijuana and coke with his druggie friends or divvied up pot to sell. The drug girls didn't hesitate to get naked right there in the house with a young boy sitting in the next room watching television. Wade had witnessed these events ever since he began visiting his dad in the summers and then living with him from the sixth grade on.

"Go to your room now, son," Dan would tell him, but the thin walls did little to mask the titillating sounds of sin throbbing in the next room.

Just when he was getting to know his nephew, Matt got pinched for a small drug deal gone bad which was added to two serious assault charges along with some misdemeanors. He was sentenced to two and a half years in prison. The sentence hit him hard. He deserved some hard time—he knew that—especially considering all the charges he'd sidestepped over the last year and things he had not been caught doing. Still, he convinced himself he'd learned all the tricks and loopholes which should have ensured he'd avoid ever being locked up again. Things beyond his control went wrong, and this time, he was going to Federal Hall instead of the first-timers' wing with the newbies.

Chapter 27
The Second Shot

Over the years, Matt had more cellmates than relatives. Some became like distant cousins whom he occasionally spotted at the liquor store or the parole office. They say you can't choose your relatives. You can't always choose your cellmates, or CMs, either, and each comes with his own stockpile of flaws and maladjustments, just like those unavoidable cousins from the backwoods whom no one wants to claim. Even so, if you can push aside the dysfunction, you often find a nugget of worth in each of them. Matt's newest roomie, Kentucky, was no exception. Kentucky was a veritable sage in his ability to tutor others in his knowledge of the streets. As a career criminal doing life plus 100 years, he had risen to a fairly respectable level in the prison hierarchy.

The prison doors at the end of the tier were opened to let in fresh air on seasonable days, but this, unfortunately, invited an influx of bugs attracted to the prison lights. Matt rolled up a newspaper he was reading and whacked a fly that landed briefly on the sink. The insect dropped dead right next to Kentucky's foot. Matt tossed the paper aside and lay back on the bed. A limp breeze made its way down to his cell along with the clamor and shouts of inmates in the yard taking advantage of rec time.

"Nope. That ain't the way you kill a fly," Kentucky drawled, reaching out his foot, stomping down hard on the lifeless bug, and giving his shoe a twist on the floor.

"That so?"

"Yep. Ever been to Rapid City?"

Matt hesitated briefly, wondering how Rapid City fit into killing flies and how much information he should divulge. "Been through there a few times." He might mention later that he'd been coming back from California or Arizona on a drug run.

"I decided to rob a convenience store there one night."

"Yeah, that happens sometimes," Matt conceded.

"I told the owner to lay down on the floor. I checked the till, and the guy only had a hundred ten bucks in the register. I'd went to all that trouble for practically nothing. I was *pissed*." Kentucky flicked the fly off the bottom of his shoe with a dirt-embedded fingernail. "It wasn't my first take in that town, and I didn't need no witnesses ratting me out, so I put a pistol to the back of his head. Damn if a spray of blood and brains didn't splatter half the store." Kentucky shook his head and let out a small chuckle. "The guy was dead, so I drove away, but lo and behold two minutes later I'm surrounded by cop cars! Turns out, after I popped him, he had enough of his marbles left to dial nine-one-one."

Out of his peripheral vision, Matt sensed Kentucky staring a hole through him, so he turned and found his instructor sitting patiently with elbows on knees and hands clasped beneath his chin, a soft, scholarly look on his face.

"So what's the lesson here?" Kentucky continued, not waiting for a reply. "I call it the philosophy of the second shot. To properly dispose of a witness or unwanted intruder, always give 'em *two* pops to the head."

Matt agreed with a blank stare. It was a type of prison code that meant he didn't disagree.

After six months, Kentucky got on Matt's nerves. The guy told the same BS stories and stunk up the cell with noxious farts no matter what he ate. He had his positive attributes: he didn't have BO, and he turned away when Matt was sitting on the can relieving himself. His least favorite CMs had been the ones with stunted social skills who continued a conversation and looked right at him while Matt shifted awkwardly on the metal toilet. Another mate had sour BO that mingled with the stink of an infrequently washed butt.

134

"You haven't been to the showers in a week," Matt prodded him every so often. "I don't miss a chance to get out of this cell for a change of scenery."

"Nah, I'm gonna try to fall asleep again."

Matt shook his head. On the inside, you didn't nag. Especially not a CM unless you were willing to come to blows. To get a point across, cracking was not only encouraged but expected. The guys who didn't shower regularly acquired names like Stinkster or Skunkster. When a newbie further down the tier asked too many bothersome questions, a short-tempered inmate yelled that he must be the president of the dumb club, and that name stuck for years. Cracking not only helped establish a pecking order but was a mental challenge to stimulate a dull environment. It complemented the art of BS'ing with its multifaceted benefits of passing the time while also creating a fiction within the boredom of reality. For a few minutes, even the lowliest could transform into a hero before it was someone else's turn to take the stage. They were actors performing monologues in front of a wary audience with a few nonfiction stories mixed into the fantasy.

While Stinkster pulled the covers over his head, a pair of guards escorted Matt and twenty-four others past the commotion of inmates readying for the day in their cells and down to the shower room. They each toted along a bar of soap in a plastic case and a mini shampoo bottle. After undressing and hanging their towels on a peg, the cons spread out in the 25x30 foot shower room. Overhead water pipes crisscrossed the room and had hundreds of small holes drilled in them. Once the men spread out under the pipes, a guard turned on a manual valve and water poured from above like a rain room. While the men soaped up, several guards stood watch outside the falling water to deter fights. Contrary to popular belief, sexual favors could be procured elsewhere, so that was not a concern, but when fistfights broke out in the shower room, the guards were faced with the difficult task of separating two slippery combatants and hauling them to the hole. The scene that followed was something like a couple of struggling farmers trying to haul away greased pigs from a muddy floor.

Chapter 28
Pedos, Rape-os, and Sickos

Career criminals, sociopaths, violent offenders, and the guy who just made a turn down the wrong path are bottled up in prison together, simmering and stewing like a toxic brew right along with the saddest of cases: those who actually need intensive mental health services. The violent offenders were no less scary behind bars, and many found the bizarre behavior of the mentally ill a form of entertainment in a place where the days dragged on endlessly. Matt developed a soft spot for LaCroix, no taller than a dresser, whiskered and with fidgety hands. He was a quiet, graying inmate who lived two cells down, and LaCroix sensed Matt's compassion. At times Matt regretted his kindness the way one does after making the mistake of feeding a stray cat. The distantness in LaCroix's eyes revealed a trampled spirit who knew the pain of madness and injustice all too well.

"Hey! Hey, bro, did you see anyone outside my cell after lights out last night? I'm ... I'm certain I heard footsteps about midnight," LaCroix said, lowering his voice to a whisper. He stroked his chin repeatedly with one hand while talking, a nervous habit Matt learned to ignore.

"No, man, I think you were safe last night," Matt reassured him. LaCroix was obsessed with the thought that a guard or inmate wanted to slide his cell door open in the dark of night and slit his throat.

"I can't take the worrying no more. I have a plan, but I can't ..." he looked around suspiciously, "I can't tell you right now," he

137

whispered, shaking his head repeatedly as though Matt were going to press for details. Then his face turned cheerless.

Matt forgot about the comment until a couple of days later when the cell doors were open for an hour, and inmates could move around the hallway.

"Hey! Hey, bro. Look at this." LaCroix unfurled his hand to reveal a wad of string. One end looped down from his hand and disappeared under his shorts. "I got it from the craft shop. See, I got the other end tied to my . . . you know." He nodded, pointing between his legs.

"You got the other end tied to your johnson?" Matt asked while the echoing clamor of dirty jokes and small-time betting weaved through the open cell doors along the tier.

"Yeah, yeah." He held the wad of string closer to Matt's face. "See, before I lay down, I'll tie this end to the cell door. That way if someone tries to open it, it'll yank me in a place I know I'll feel and wake right up! It's foolproof!"

"Okay," Matt said. If it gave LaCroix peace of mind, what would it hurt? Matt empathized. He slept fitfully and had been plagued with nightmares for as long as he could remember, so he understood the unease that came with darkness. Besides, LaCroix was easier to deal with than the nutty inmates who screamed for hours at night or even howled. There was no way to escape those sounds in a cell. Sometimes the screeching sounds were a comfort in a twisted way. *At least I'm not that messed up. There's hope for me.* It broke the monotony as well, and anything that made life bearable even for a short time was worth it.

Contraband was the best distraction. It was usually passed along during visitation. The South Dakota State Penitentiary had a minimum contact policy. A visiting wife or girlfriend could give a hug, quick kiss, and then sit side-by-side with the inmate holding hands. Even with many guards watching, it was possible to pass along drugs.

Drugs weren't the only contraband. There was a long list of banned items that could send an inmate to the hole for an extended stay. A popular but forbidden valuable was hot wires that could be rigged into a cell outlet and used to boil water. In winter, the air was perpetually damp-cold so anything warmer than the thin institutional blankets was welcome. Soup and hot chocolate were banned treats which made them all the more desirable on a frigid day when there was nothing to do but stare endlessly at blank walls. Like any prison, the guards regularly searched for these banned items.

Sometimes if an inmate had been tipped off that a search was about to happen word would spread through the cell blocks. Then it was time to hide the weapons, drugs, pornography, hot wires, and other illegal items. Large items could be given to a friend in another block or stashed out of the cell in a shop or kitchen where the prisoners worked until the shakedown ended. There was always the risk of not getting the goods back, but it was better than getting busted.

Other times a shakedown came without warning. Three officers would come down the tier, remove everyone from a cell into a holding area, and probe the cell by lifting the mattresses, looking under the rim of the toilet, shining a flashlight down the sink drain, and using a mirror to check under surfaces that could have a hidden blade. Then the prisoners in the adjacent cells would have to "suitcase" small items or get caught with them and head to the hole. The items were placed in a plastic bag which was inserted into the rectum, thus suitcased, until the search was over. One of Matt's cellmates kept a five-inch shampoo bottle supplied by the prison and filled it with his beloved hot wires and other contraband which he suitcased on a regular basis.

Afterward, while they put their cells back together, they commiserated about what a******s the guards were for treating them like scum and coming into their personal living spaces like they owned the place. Besides the fact that pretty much everyone on the inside claimed to be innocent, they shared a hatred for authority and the legal system. In the distance, someone swore loudly about his belongings "being thrown all over hell."

Matt's CM yanked one of the strewn sheets back onto his mattress and snorted. "If I went through their personal belongings like that I'd be charged with a crime."

"My best dream would be to take a cop, a judge, and a D.A. and bring them to an abandoned farm where I could hook up a sewer pipe right over their heads and then incarcerate *them* for a few weeks. That might make them think twice about handing out these big sentences they like to toss around. They ain't got no idea what it's like in here." Matt picked up a bookmark that had fallen to the floor and thumbed through his *True West* book trying to find where he left off.

He did most of his reading in the relative silence of the law library though. A lifer who worked there, Smiley, knew every book in the place from years of trying to find a way to appeal his own sentence. He could lead anyone to the right source if he wanted to, though he rarely did. The court-appointed lawyers who represented most of the men on the inside had such heavy caseloads they couldn't spend much time researching cases. So Matt spent his extra time reading Supreme Court rulings and anything else to help him understand the purpose of certain laws or to find a way to appeal based on similar cases. He didn't find an out, and perhaps for most of them, the wild chase offered hope more than actual success. Yet it became a game of wits in which the benefit of time would ultimately give him an advantage over the prison officials years down the road. At least for a while.

On the inside, there was no bourbon to boil his blood, which meant that Matt didn't go looking for fights. Almost everyone learned their boundaries quickly, but occasionally it came to blows over disrespect. These brawls were street fights, not boxing matches. The only rule being that there were no rules, but that rule could change. Would the other guy be coming at you with a shank, rocks in a sock, or a real weapon?

One morning a guy down the tier started shouting for spare magazines or newspapers. His cellmate, a new fish, made the mistake of bragging to a lifer and then disrespecting the guy, and now had an appointment to pay for his crime. Matt ignored the request, but during open tier time, he walked down and watched the fish's cellmate help him strap layers of magazines to his chest and stomach as body armor.

140

"This guy you dissed has some real connections," the cellmate warned him.

Clearly Fish wanted to turn back the hands of time, but if he didn't fight, he'd drop to the bottom of the pecking order, which was a fate worse than death. Word spread through the cells, and nearly every inmate on the row gathered to watch the fight that was scheduled to take place at the end of the hall by the stairway, a place out of view of the guards. The lifer had muscular shoulders, long, slicked-back hair, and was covered in homemade tattoos, one a swastika on the side of his neck. Fish showed up with newspaper wrapped around his arms and covered by a long-sleeved shirt and a telephone book secured by string across his abdomen. Fish had no weapon other than a couple of sharp pencils he scrounged up. The lifer had a piece of razor-sharp chrome given to him by a con wanting to score a favor and silently came after Fish with his hand raised. Fish stood frozen at first, then tried to back away, but the crowd pushed him back toward the lifer, who shoved the scrappy but outranked guy to the floor.

"Stab that f***er!" someone yelled. The mob of inmates pressed in until Fish's back was against the wall. When the lifer started gouging chunks out of Fish's unprotected neck and face, Fish came wailing and flailing to life. His screams and the roar of cons cheering on the lifer brought the guards running, but they had to force their way through the tight group of men intent on watching some excitement. The guards eventually took the lifer to the hole and Fish to the prison hospital.

"Blessed is he who's smart enough not to trust anyone in this place," Matt said, brandishing a hand around the room in response to Mary's latest claim that "blessed is the one who trusts in God."

"You're not *like* these other people," she said with such conviction Matt almost believed her but instead grilled her about how much time she wasted with the other church ladies. Here was Mary, the only person who ever showed true concern for him, and how did he repay her? With sarcasm and unnecessary hurtful comments. Sure, what set him apart from the other inmates was that they all *believed* they didn't deserve to be here. Matt *knew* this wasn't where he belonged. If he'd had the money for a better lawyer, he would have never seen the inside of these walls. Still, with his street smarts, he was able to blend in which made life easier. He couldn't say the same for the Hutterites who shared the next cell. With their odd dress code and thick German accents, they were oddly out of place in this violent prison atmosphere, looking as though they'd taken a wrong turn on the way to worship and ended up here. Their perpetual prayers filtered into Matt's cell. If they weren't praying, they were talking quietly, sometimes in German, always about God or faith. They rarely left their cell during tier time. The father and son wore traditional full beards and black pants with their peculiar lack of back pockets. Prison code didn't allow for the traditional suspenders, but they were allowed white, button-down shirts with collars. Both were serving time for the white-collar crime of defrauding a bank. They'd procured massive loans for cattle, then sold the cattle and not repaid the loans.

"I hear they've sentencing guidelines now, but when we were charged, they didn't," the son told Matt on one of his rare forays into the hallway during tier time.

"I admitted to the judge that I had sinned against man and God and to charge me as he saw fit. He sentenced me to ten years."

"Oh yeah? I thought your old man said he was in for longer than that."

"Yes, well, when my father approached the judge, he forgot his peaceful ways and shouted, *"You can't judge me! You are only a man! Only God can judge me!"* The young man cast his saddened eyes downward. "The judge sentenced him to *twenty* years. For the exact same crime!"

Chapter 29
Revolving Door

After three years on the inside, he'd be released tomorrow. Mary would pick him up and bring him to Dan's, where he'd stay until who-knew-when. Incarceration had changed his thought process, causing him to remain rooted to the dysfunctional life necessary for prison survival. Transitioning from a snake hole back into freedom should have been a snap, yet the disparity of the settings made it both painful and restorative. Matt lay on the bunk staring at the ceiling where years of seepage left pockmarks of paint scattered across it like a disease, one that spread and contaminated the souls of the men within as if through cosmic diffusion. Matt entered tough and independent but now felt as hard as the steel and stone that kept him from society.

He spent weeks anticipating the moment when the prison would disappear in the side view mirror, and the open window would bathe his face with the winds of freedom. Yet once inside Dan's square white house surrounded by homes that would have been considered moderate fifty years ago, he gravitated quickly to the bedroom. It was difficult to determine whether it was day or night since Matt kept the heavy curtains pulled tight at all times.

"Are you ever coming outta that stinkin' room?" Dan asked, rapping on the spare bedroom door where Matt was now living. There was no answer. "You ain't in prison no more. You can come out. See a little sunshine or something; pink up that pasty skin of yours." He waited a moment before throwing his arms up and returning to the business of dividing a sack of marijuana into $40 bags at the kitchen table while a frozen TV dinner whirred in the microwave.

Matt scurried for the shallow waters of the familiar the first few days after his release. Gradually he edged toward the murky depths. Friends were jubilant he'd been released, so it was hard to explain the anxiety that accompanied this new freedom; his new unknown. He was like a pet store fish that had to first sit in its plastic bag and adjust to the temperature of its new home. The longer he was in, the harder it was to readjust to the outside. The other day he tagged along with Dan to Walmart, then sat in the car skittish as a kitten, too hesitant to mingle with these unfamiliar people when he was used to seeing the same faces in the same places for years.

After a week he ventured onto the front lawn, newly green with weeds and grass and not too overdue for a cut. He jerked a dented lawnmower through a barricade of leftover plywood and stacked boxes of what he presumed to be broken junk, then pulled the starter a good dozen times, each "jerk'" encouraged with an expletive. When the ancient beast buzzed to life, he quickly mowed the front lawn. The backyard was dry dirt courtesy of Dan's pit bull, Otis, who had scraped his chain relentlessly from fence to fence.

Though spring was just settling in, sweat dripped down his chest as though it were August, and his heart pounded dangerously fast. After shoving the mower back in the garage, he spent the rest of the week holed up in his room, only grunting a response whenever a ringing phone was followed by Dan shouting, "Casper, telephone!" Then adding, when Matt failed to respond, "Should I tell them you're busy painting your nails?"

The two hadn't been in a physical fight since their late teens. They'd frequently argued ever since, but it never lasted. Matt came out of his room and accused Dan of becoming an ass when he drank.

"Right back at ya," Dan had said, shifting and budging his wheelchair through the door frame in an attempt to get outside and end the fight.

"Don't let the wheelchair stop you," Matt called after him.

Too much time to lie around thinking consumed Matt with worry about breaking parole the way a neighbor on his tier did and came traipsing right back in for another year. Being on parole meant going to a nightclub was forbidden, and he was determined to follow the rules. Yet within a month, shrouded in a haze of cigarette smoke, he was lined up behind a pool cue plotting how to fence some stolen goods he'd traded for drugs that afternoon.

"This inner cop-radar you think you have is broken," Dan said smugly, satisfied with his own conservative plan to only sell drugs and only to certain people. He didn't believe in branching out. "You can't get by on hunches forever."

"I ain't gonna live my life looking over my shoulder like a scared little kitten."

"Only an idiot isn't afraid. You have to keep your guard up."

But Matt did get by on instinct. He could read people, and his boldness threw them. He strode confidently into any setting as though he belonged there when people were on the lookout for a shifty-eyed grease ball looking over his shoulder. It wasn't so much ESP as being able to size up personalities and the best angles. He'd been perfecting this since his junior high days when he noticed how eager many gas station attendants were to parade their mechanical knowledge. He also realized why the expression *a partner in crime* was so commonplace. The best scams required a buddy, so Matt corralled a friend to drop him off a block from a gas station with a lone attendant to pull what he called his *till tap*. Matt would hand the attendant five bucks, ask for change for the vending machine, and watch which button the guy pushed to open the till. Then he'd browse at something until the friend pulled in exactly five minutes later, put up the hood of the car, and came in to ask the attendant to come listen to a nonexistent noise in the engine. When the attendant's nose was buried in the car, Matt would tap the button to open the till, remove a few tens and twenties without leaving any of the trays empty, and then walk off. It had worked for years now with the exception of one time a second employee appeared out of nowhere while Matt's hand was in the till. *What the hell are you doing?* the guy asked, to which Matt had mumbled that he was

145

making change for a five and then hustled out of there with his head down.

When he was off parole, his life again became a revolving cycle of arrests, fights, multiple stints in the county jail, and more arrests. He took up where he left off with Dan, starting the cycle all over. He accumulated more charges for multiple assaults, eluding, and a DUI. He prided himself on learning from past mistakes and continually improving his game while in fact, he was unable to learn from experience or he'd have stopped.

The state's attorney barely bothered to glance at Matt. Matt, on the other hand, never failed to take into account his surroundings and began silently judging this dour prosecutor who was thumbing through a folder of papers, too arrogant to feel shame over his middle-aged pot belly or piggy eyes set behind what he must have considered smart-looking glasses. Matt gritted his teeth when the man stood to begin his tirade.

"Your honor, I want the court to know exactly who this individual is. The man seated before you," he swept a steady hand toward Matt in what seemed an embarrassingly dramatic Perry Mason impersonation, "has been arrested more times than any other person in the history of Minnehaha County, quite possibly the entire state, and is not yet even thirty years old. He is a habitual criminal who is unable to conform to the rules of society."

The judge's eyes met Matt's. In contrast to the court-appointed lawyer who didn't seem to care whether or not Matt ended up in prison, the state's attorney had done his homework and discovered a rap sheet of over forty arrests. The judge said *enough*, and with no sentencing guidelines at the time, sentenced him to five years.

"Those damn judges hand out years like they're handing out party favors," Matt griped upon having to once again store his meager possessions and head to the Big House. This time he sold his prized car and motorcycle knowing he'd need lots of commissary money in the years to come. He left society on a cloudy fall day, and it was during this stretch which began in 1990 when Matt felt he melded with the prison. He knew its cryptic corners, its secrets, its weaknesses, and he exploited each one of these to rise to the top of the prisoner hierarchy.

Years ago, on his first stretch in, he made the same mistakes as most first-timers. He entered scared but with a chip on his shoulder and left well-versed in the soul-sapping rhythm of prison life. The second time through, the violence, boredom, and dreariness only fueled his hatred of others. Each day was a dysfunctional replay of the one before. The third time was certain to be the charm. He was determined to find a way to rise above it. That's because he was above it all, not your ordinary con. He waited for an opportunity to present her face. She always did eventually.

Until then, he would continue to watch and learn. He processed and interpreted every detail, even the fact that the cells had all been painted "colors that calm." Sickly pale green or mustardy brown. It didn't work though. Out on the tier, two inmates postured like polecats and spewed vulgar threats: *Don't turn your back on me for the next two years, f*****! I know what your p**** a** did!* Farther down, a guy pulled his T-shirt completely over his eyes and appeared to be mumbling to himself, completely unaware of the chaos around him. A bald guy who was playing cards had a freshly broken nose. The nose fit the look, and the game went on. Some of the only escapes from this chaos were homemade booze and smuggled in drugs, and Matt's new CM happened to be a prison moonshiner.

Inmates who worked in the kitchen, like Matt's CM, had access to the ingredients needed for the prison wine. He stole fruit, usually oranges and fruit cocktail, and added in some sugar, something acidic like vinegar, and finally yeast or even bread. This would be mixed together in a big plastic bag and set somewhere warm, usually under the bunk. During the cold parts of the year, he babied that bag like a sickly animal by constantly covering it with warm towels throughout the day. At the end of the week, the mushy fruit was squeezed out, and a foul-tasting substance called pruno was ready to drink.

"This hooch is a big step down for me," his CM said, taking a shut-eyed whiff of the noxious liquid. "I made big money. I mean big. I had a big business doin' these big money deals. All the bigwigs in town came to me 'cause they knew I could get the job done." He snapped his fingers. "I'd turn a paltry hundred thou into some real big money like that if you know what I mean."

Matt knew exactly what he meant. *Everyone in here is innocent and rich, but can you borrow me ten bucks for the commissary?* The commissary provided the basics for the prison bartering system. Inmates were only allowed $35 per month in a commissary account, and this money could be used to buy candy bars, potato chips, cigarettes, or even cans of tobacco and rolling paper. Some inmates had no one to put money into their account or lost commissary privileges due to getting written up for fighting or being insubordinate to a guard. They often resorted to brewing pruno in order to have some bartering power.

"I still got these big bank accounts all over the state. When I blow this joint, I'll go back to drinking only the finest whiskey, straight up, like the old days."

"Yeah, I'm a Jim Beam guy myself. On the rocks. What kind of fancy whiskey did you drink?"

His CM hesitated and appeared to purposely almost drop the valuable liquid as a decoy. "I, uh, well . . ." Of course, he couldn't name one. "Uh—hey! You wanna buy some hooch from me? Since you're my CM, I'll cut you a deal. Twenty bucks for enough to get you drunk."

"I'll pass. I'd rather stay sober than drink that poison."

When the CM lost his job in the kitchen, he resorted to brewing up some potato hooch. It was a slightly different process. He capped the container with a balloon but let it sit too long, and one boring afternoon the concoction blew up, and potato flew through the cell as though it had been spattered from a paintball gun. A lot of cons brewed the stuff, and the guards turned a blind eye unless there was a shakedown. Or if the hooch blew up all over the cell. The guy was sent to the hole for thirty days, which gave Matt a one-month reprieve from the endless fabrications about million-dollar business deals.

Chapter 30
Companionship

Matt feared the unknown, and every trip to prison meant entering uncharted territory. Surprisingly, the rules had changed for the better while he was gone. The new warden also believed in allowing the prisoners some autonomy. One welcome change was that there was no longer a lights-out rule. Inmates could stay up all night if desired. Matt was a night owl, so he relished this freedom. He fell into a routine of plugging in his headphones at 10 PM when it became a requirement to turn off the volume, and then unplugging them from his little black-and-white television about midnight. It left enough time to sleep and still get up for breakfast.

When he finally went to bed, the flashes of light from the other TV sets up and down the block gave a strobe light effect, making it difficult to sleep. The lights were never turned off in the cells, but blackness from the outer windows gave a softer effect than daylight. He pulled the itchy state-issued blanket over his head to block out the brightness, but the heat became stifling. Had it been winter, he'd have welcomed the extra warmth to stave off the radiating chill that pierced the drafty stone building. Today the building had grown suffocatingly hot, and for relief, the guards opened the doors at the end of the block that led into the prison yard. With no screen, however, insects swarmed in. Matt untangled his arms from the blanket and swatted at a couple of flies buzzing relentlessly. It was a matter of a hot blanket or biting insects.

Laardvark, Matt's new CM, was snoring unmercifully loud in the bunk below him. Laardvark acquired this name after once talking about eating lard sandwiches as a kid. Someone couldn't resist noting that the fat stuck with him and added that he *didn't grow that stomach overnight*. He was not only wide but short and had a long, beaked nose, yet took pride in being called Laardvark.

"It seemed like in high school everyone had a nickname but me. I never fit in there, but now I feel like part of a team. You know, the Tier Two Team," he said, indicating their cell on the second floor.

Laardvark could sleep through anything. Matt hopped down and smacked blindly at the buzzing sounds in the flickering light that was too bright to sleep but too dim to illuminate a small, black insect. After accomplishing nothing but knocking over a book, the noise miraculously stopped, and he'd just lain back down when a sickly, low moan shivered into the cell from a few doors down. Matt swore, turned one ear to the pillow, and pulled to his other ear a wadded up blanket that smelled of the crumbling mortar and mold that permeated the prison. He braced himself for the shrieks that were certain to follow. Once Wacko started his nighttime howling, he wouldn't gear down until morning. After several attempts at bending his elbow at just the right angle to hold the wad of fabric against his ear without having his arm fall asleep, perspiration began dripping into his eye.

"Damn it!" Matt smacked his pillow against the wall, which sent the cup at the foot of his bed crashing to the ground and got the flies buzzing again. Laardvark woke up with an ear-cracking snort.

"That motherf***er needs to get his f***ing head screwed on right," Laardvark croaked in his state of half-sleep.

Matt sank back into the pillow, clenched his eyes, and squeezed the smelly blanket tighter to his ear. He thought of LaCroix and the other crazies, as most of the inmates called them.

"Thank God I have my sanity," Matt mumbled. If there was someone smart enough to philosophize with, he'd have asked them their thoughts on why some people in life have to suffer so much through no fault of their own. Some people, like him, got dealt the crap hand in life's poker game. Then Matt surprised himself with some charitable thoughts about the unfairness of LaCroix's suffering and inexplicably fell into the first deep sleep he had since arriving here.

"Damn it." He woke up the next morning itching three red mosquito bites on his face and arms.

"Got bit up last night, bro? Did a skeeter get yer peter?" Laardvark laughed hysterically at his childish rhyme.

Surprisingly, Laardvark was up. He was one of the few obese guys Matt had ever known who was too lazy to go eat and during breakfast generally lay cocooned in his blankets like a fleshy vampire. The dude apparently absorbed calories from the air. He pushed past Matt and stuffed a two-inch square of toast into a baggie that he carefully rolled up and placed under his pillow. "I need it for later. Don't touch it."

"As if." Matt sat on the one chair and stretched the newspaper across the tiny table. After what must have been an exhausting breakfast, Laardvark was soon snoring away the rest of the morning. The man didn't have a single redeeming quality. He was a self-centered windbag. On the inside, inmates are allowed few possessions and often became very possessive of what they do have. Most didn't long for more than a relationship. A closeness with someone they could love or if not love at least trust a little.

"This here's for my pet." Laardvark nodded toward the corner when he awoke later.

"Your what?"

"I got a mouse that keeps coming to visit every night. I'm training him."

"You think you can train a mouse?"

"I done it before. It's kinda my specialty. See, I always had a dog growing up. Even if we was living out of the car, the dog came with us. It was my stepdad's only good quality that he liked animals." He grunted hard, bending down to lay a mini-trail of six toast crumbs leading to the bunk. The effort he took to accomplish this small feat rivaled Matt's sixty-minute weight-lifting routine. "Yeah, even my foster parents had two dogs."

Matt nodded and thought back to his own stepdad's lack of admirable attributes.

"Rufus was the best. I trained him to roll over, crawl on his belly, jump over a stack of beer cans, and fetch a pack of cigarettes off the shelf."

Sometimes the memories came back like a sucker punch. *Stepdad. Beer cans. Cigarettes. Foster family.* Matt's head buzzed with the sickening memories. He had a sudden urge to punch something, and his CM's rambling voice faded into the background.

"HEY! I said how about you?" Laardvark almost shouted.

"What's that?"

"I said, did you ever have a dog?"

"Yeah, for about a week. It was—"

Laardvark held a hand up to silence Matt and leaned over with his large stomach hanging earthward like a swollen bag. "Tch tch tch." He let out a soft mouse-call, the only gentle action Matt ever witnessed from him, and his eyes grew wider with each forward scuttle of the mouse until it finally squeaked its way to the bunk. The enormous man bent down with an outstretched hand containing a pea-sized morsel that he placed on the ground. Matt sat mesmerized as the little creature scuttled around the floor by their feet, apparently unaware that the two men in his midst had no conscience.

The mouse returned frequently, but it wasn't enough to counter Laardvark's many annoying traits, so Matt plotted the next move with the expertise of a chess master; it was a necessity for life on the inside, and the weak or weak-minded were quickly dealt with.

Education wasn't as highly valued among inmates as the street smarts that got you through each day, and right now Matt's priority for getting through the day was getting a new CM before he ended up smacking Laardvark and ending up in the hole. The warden wouldn't be moved by Matt's unhappiness with the guy's laziness or the fact that he repeated the same blow-hard stories nearly every night. What the warden cared about was discipline and personal progress. In fact, by now Matt had become accustomed to the guy's smell much in the same way he hardly noticed the way the tier was overcome with powerful smells emanating from countless toilets being filled and flushed every morning. The revolting stench diffused into the haze of cigarette smoke and body odors to create an unholy stink that lingered around the clock. Once when the walls were being painted, the oily fumes provided a welcome relief from the usual odor.

Matt requested an application for a new CM and explained in writing how he and Laardvark had almost gotten into physical confrontations, and more importantly that this guy refused to better himself. *My cellmate's insistence on lying in his bunk smoking all day and putting no effort toward becoming a productive citizen is hindering the progress I've made toward rehabilitation.* It was expected that after a few months one of the CMs would request a change until they found someone they could live with. For a while anyway. After two people had been cooped up together for months on end, the little annoyances became unbearable. After a few weeks, Matt got the word. He'd been in for six months with no write-ups and was rewarded with a single cell. It was the prison equivalent of winning the lottery.

Chapter 31
Movie Night

Entertainment was at a premium in this house of monotony. Infrequent opportunities for true competition meant that game night was anticipated with the vigor of a back alley street fight. It wasn't uncommon for someone to get beaten or even shanked over a game of Monopoly. Aside from some occasional fistfights, however, the prison had been operating smoothly with no stabbings or murders. Because of this, the administration decided that one time per week they would show a movie to the inmates via the cable television system that could be viewed on the small black-and-white TV set that each cell contained. This worked well for several weeks, and the promise of an entertaining movie to break the unbearable boredom was a powerful incentive not to get written up. Apparently, no one considered the careful planning required in choosing a movie within an ecosystem containing hundreds of violent individuals packed together under a depressing cloud of tension. Tempers could ignite in seconds.

One evening, the movie *American Me* played on the fuzzy little TV sets throughout the prison. The movie depicts the fictional account of the founding and rise to power of the Mexican Mafia in the California prison system. When the gang members in the movie began throwing out racial slurs, the inmates who were watching the show began shouting taunts of disrespect toward rival gangs and enemies as well. The friction continued throughout the night.

When the bell sounded to open the doors in the morning, some convicts headed to the cafeteria packing homemade weapons and carefully eyeing the inmates they thought had thrown them disrespect the night before. Matt felt the grim tension, and the sickening feeling—the calm before the storm—did not go unnoticed. He sat down close to an exit with his smaller than usual breakfast. The absence of the usual noise and clatter resulted in a prickle of unease settling in his stomach. He noticed the threatening looks, posturing, and quick, aggressive movements. The tension billowed, filling the room like a thunderhead. Suddenly, some shouts were exchanged a few tables down, and two guards snapped to attention, moving in the direction of what was clearly becoming a hostile situation. Before they could react, expletives filled the room, and a pitiful scream punctuated the explosion of tempers. In a matter of seconds, confusion erupted, and some people ran toward the screams while others ran away from them. Hidden by a wall of frenzied men, a Mexican gang member repeatedly plunged a long, chrome shank that he smuggled from the auto body shop into his rival. The victim was blocked in and had no means of defense. He left his cell confident that this gang member was all talk and threats and would never carry through on the warning he gave last night during the movie.

The inmates responded to the guards' shouts to move away, and the crowd finally cleared to reveal a still body lying in a pool of blood. The man was dead, and the prison went on immediate lockdown. After that, there were no more cinematic rewards. All of it sparked by an inappropriate movie choice.

Chapter 32
The Small Business Owner

A year into the five-year sentence of his third maximum security stretch, Matt achieved trustee status. His five-year sentence allowed just enough time for the darkness and vice to fester together in a pot of maladjustment. Matt got a job as a cook for the prison staff. Before this, Matt, who thrived on thrill-seeking, sought out a job that offered at least a snippet of liberty and had soon earned a job as a runner on the tier. This meant that his cell door was always open so he could run errands for the lieutenant or correctional officers. Other than having to be in his cell for lockup or count, he had the leniency to go about the prison to deliver messages and such. This often required going past the staff break room where a soda machine sat just inside the door practically begging him to use his vending machine trick to jimmy out a Coke whenever the room was empty. The job had other perks as well, allowing him to mosey about while on errands and usually managing to snag a snack from the kitchen crew. He soon got caught stealing soda and lost the coveted job but was quickly able to earn trustee status nonetheless due to not getting any write-ups.

Extensive knowledge of prison operations helped him incubate a plan to run a drug operation into the main compound. The plan began when he moved into the trustee cottage, which was part of the prison grounds yet not part of the main prison building. The kitchen where he was assigned to work also wasn't located inside the main compound, yet it shared a wall with the maximum

157

security prison. This common wall contained a heavy locked steel door that led to a hallway, which led to an adjoining room with a wall of telephones that inmates could use to make calls. Matt noticed that a gap beneath this door would allow a manila envelope to be slid into the hallway. Bingo. Opportunity practically leaped into his arms.

While standing in front of an industrial oven cooking ground beef in a skillet, he began hatching a plan. He did his best work while multi-tasking and tossed a mound of cumin atop the beef, not bothering to measure since the combination of an artistic eye and years of weighing out baggies of pot gave him the ability to judge such things accurately. The creativity involved in preparing the ingredients inspired him, and each can of crushed tomatoes or heap of diced onions brought with it a piece of the plan until by the end of his shift he had created not only a steaming pot of chili but a way to make life on the inside more palatable. There were just a few kinks to work out.

Matt's mind had whirred in constant motion during his waking hours for as long as he could remember. If he had nothing to think about, he turned edgy. He attended to detail with the precision of a machine and thought several steps ahead in the manner of a chess master. In less than a week, he masterminded a plan to make a healthy profit by bringing marijuana into the prison. Both money and being in control filled his need for power, and this near-obsession with organizing a drug ring finally bloomed into a workable scheme. The missing piece, a trustable person on the inside, presented himself in the form of Matt's old acquaintance, an unshakeable lifer who was trustable in the "let's not con each other, and we can both benefit" sense. The guy had respect on the inside, was tight-mouthed, and most importantly was serving a life sentence. Matt considered all possible scenarios and settled on the one where he'd make less money but have less risk due to the small number of people who would be involved.

The idea had germinated years ago in the county jail when guys on work release would return with joints they either smoked or sold for an outrageous sum. What sprung the idea to life was a simple gap beneath a door. Within a month, this drug ring into the prison was in full swing. Matt analyzed every detail to reduce the obvious risks, but of course, you could never completely trust anyone.

Matt sat on the steps of the trustee cottage, hidden by shadows and blessed by cloud cover that muted a bright moon. He should have felt butterflies or at least some hesitation, but his plan was perfect, and he felt that useless worries and anxieties only brought fear to life. He listened for the sound of an engine slowing, and when he heard it at the exact time he'd prearranged with his friend, he allowed himself a small smile. This friend from the outside drove past and threw something out of the car window. It landed with a soft bounce on the curb. Matt casually walked over by the street and picked up the bag of drugs from the ground, slipped it under his jacket, and walked straight into the trustee kitchen.

Generally, there were other trustees in the kitchen where he worked preparing meals for the guards. Tonight, though, he arranged to do the evening prep work for tomorrow's meals, which gave him an excuse to be alone in the kitchen, where he used a rolling pin to crush the marijuana flat before pouring the fine crumbs into an envelope. He flipped the radio onto a rock station and waited for 7 PM to roll around. Matt's biggest safety net was that he relied on only one person as his link to the inside; his old acquaintance from the library, the lifer. Certainly, *friend* was too strong of a word, but considering the choices for camaraderie behind bars, the guy was passable. There was something off about him, but then that pretty much described everyone on the inside. He was serving a life sentence for a violent rape, a crime that put him mid-range on the unspoken "crime respectability" ladder. It wasn't an offense as admirable as cop-killing yet nothing that was considered much worse than what anyone else in the general population had done. He spent his days looking for a loophole or way out of the joint, eventually earning a job in the law library. Over the years he grew as quiet and serious as the scholarly books that he watched over with the attentiveness of a new mother. Even his features became as stiff as the hardcovers of the legal tomes with their multisyllabic words, earning him the ironic nickname *Smiley*.

He gave Matt information on more than one occasion. "One piece of advice. The bigger the word, the better. Long words build long sentences, and that means you'll probably confuse someone. You got to know your Latin words in order to impress," he said, twisting in the chair to heave his walrus-sized stomach into a more comfortable position. "*Suvoir dire* won't get you anywhere. Confusion equals chaos, and chaos equals victory."

It was some of the best legal advice Matt ever received on the inside, and he had an extensive vocabulary, though he knew better than to use it. Guys in here weren't interested in intellectually stimulating conversations as much as cracking, still one of Matt's favorite pastimes, which was why he was more likely to find himself discussing how Smiley looked like a rat that had swallowed a beanbag. The current warden still had an all-you-can-eat policy during meals, and Smiley took full advantage of this deal.

For reasons no one knew for sure, Smiley either had an in with the guards, or they chose to turn the other way as long as there was no trouble when he had runners smuggle him meat from the kitchen so he could cook burgers on his illegal hot plate. The cells would fill with the aroma of the sizzling meat, and he sold the burgers for $3 each. The fact that Smiley could get away with things that others couldn't increased the faith Matt had in choosing him as a business partner, though, on the other hand, it left lingering doubts about what information or services Smiley provided that allowed him to earn this favor with the staff.

Still, the fewer people involved in the new plan meant there were fewer people who could get caught and then snitch out the others for a reduced sentence. In choosing someone serving a life sentence, Matt found someone who couldn't bargain for a lighter sentence in exchange for turning in information about the drug ring. When he first asked the lifer to be his partner-in-crime, Smiley answered with a typical corpse-cold response: "Maybe." The man was sinister but tight-lipped. It was as foolproof a system as possible, especially considering that others suspected Smiley had connections to a lieutenant he once blackmailed who was known to take bribes from inmates. The lifer had good behavior and had put in for a monthly pass to use the payphone at 7 PM.

Right on time, Matt heard a rap on the steel door, which was his signal to slip the envelope under the gap. This lifer picked up the envelope on the other side, and Matt felt that same adrenaline surge he got from flooring the gas pedal of a racecar or unleashing his anger in a barroom brawl. His drug of choice wasn't a drug at all but rather conning, duping, and manipulating, and this fix would only last a few hours before he'd be jonesing for another scam.

Although Matt had trustee status and lived outside of the main prison, he had the legal right to access and use the law library which happened to be where the lifer worked. After a pat-down, a guard allowed Matt access into the prison and the library, a room frequented by inmates attempting to help with their own appeal processes or working to get their case overturned. Matt was no stranger to this room, having looked up cases to support his own parole. No one ever wrote him a letter of support to present to the parole board, and he never asked for one, preferring to look for cases to support his release instead. Matt grabbed the nearest book from a shelf and walked over to the lifer, who already saw him but left the fact unacknowledged.

"I need a pound," he said to Matt in a low whisper. "My ol' lady put the cash in your account last week." Matt nodded. He'd have Dan check his bank balance first, but so far the guy hadn't tried to scam him. Every month Smiley let Matt know what time his phone pass was for, and Matt would prepare the green wonder weed for the envelope. Cash never exchanged hands, and Matt started earning $2,000 to $3,000 per month from the safety of his cell. It took meticulous planning and steel-belted nerves to organize this drug trade inside the most secure institute in the state of South Dakota, and Matt did it successfully.

Once a month Matt had the opportunity to earn a twelve-hour furlough through good behavior. It was an opportunity for inmates to gradually earn small freedoms in order to increase their likelihood of staying out of trouble once they were finally released from prison. Matt sat on the steps of the cottage, knowing Dan would pick him up on time as always. They'd go to his house, and then he'd return Matt right on time—along with a pound of pot that Matt could carry right into the trustee cottage as there was no search or pat-down in this area of the prison. It had been foolproof until last week.

"Those nosy f****** sealed off my door," he said, sliding into the passenger's seat of Dan's car.

"What door?"

"The one between the kitchen and the hallway that has the gap under it. I heard that the goons got word something was going on, but they couldn't catch us, so they just sealed it off." Actually, someone heard that the guards were smelling marijuana frequently near the cells and were suspicious, so they started asking around until they found a snitch, but the snitch didn't have enough information since no one knew the ins and outs of the plan besides Matt and the lifer.

"At least you're lucky they didn't catch you. I'm thinking you should be happy about that!" Dan's eyes pleaded.

"F*** that! I'm making good money, and I ain't giving up the money without a fight. There's got to be another way."

"You're six months from getting out. Maybe it's time to just wait it out and be patient." Dan pulled into his driveway and removed some letters from the mailbox before heading inside.

"Nah, patient ain't never worked for me," Matt said, knowing that if he quit he'd be just like every other con, and he had a deep-seated need to be the top dog, to feel superior to the others. Besides,

Dan had just given an idea for a new plan. All Matt would have to do is talk to his neighbor in the trustee cottage tomorrow.

"What I need," he said to this neighbor while setting the weights down, "is a . . ." he faltered as if the word he needed lay on the rec floor of a grimy prison, " . . . someone who has access to move about the prison." This man, whose job was to deliver mail to the inmates, had coincidentally lived next to him in the maximum security area as well, and they still lifted weights together. He was a slyly deceitful, middle-aged con with a hard-earned reputation throughout the prison among those drawn to his gift for knowing everything that was happening on the inside. There was no deep friendship between the two; after all, you could hardly scrape up a crumb of trust around this place, but compared to most, he was reliable enough to take a chance.

"Like the mailman?" his friend said, immediately onto Matt's plan.

"There's not much risk. I've been doing this for months already." Matt was persuasive, and by the time the last weight hit the floor, the mailman was in. A stream of sweat rolled down both sides of Matt's face. He pumped these weights religiously for at least forty-five minutes, five days a week. Strength was a necessity, not an option. Weakness could mean the difference between life and death, which Matt found ironic. The system that tried to prevent inmates from getting hurt allowed them to muscle up, which resulted in a population of inmates that were not only violent and crazy but also strong enough to snap someone's neck.

The new plan was foolproof. The mailman had been delivering mail inside for years and was in and out of the prison so often that he was never searched upon entering. To deliver mail, he used a vending tray with straps that went over his shoulder like the kind used to sell popcorn and peanuts at a baseball game. He filled the tray with mail and now would just have one more envelope in his tray; the one that was filled with pot. Matt added one more safeguard. He addressed the envelope to the warden. If a guard

163

ever decided to check through the mail, he wouldn't dare to open something addressed to the warden. He still sold to his friend in the law library but now had the ability to sell to a couple of other lifers as well. Business soared.

First, the lifers got their envelopes. Then they used a Chapstick lid as their unit of measurement, and each cap cost $25. Each ounce of pot was divided into sixty to seventy capfuls, resulting in astronomical profits but with much more risk. This mailman was serving a short sentence which made him a risk if he got caught with the weed, but there was no other way to deliver to so many people. Besides, the mailman knew everyone, and if a shakedown was going to take place, he was always one of the first to hear about it. The system worked without a hiccup. There was too much mail to sort through, and no one ever questioned an envelope addressed to the warden.

"Eight more days and I'll be buying a Suzuki big block and cruising the streets instead of stuck in this dingy house, Shorty," Matt said with an upward inflection in his voice. Then he reached over and patted Dan's head. His older brother pulled away.

"Good for you, jailbird."

But they were empty words, just little attacks in a brotherly game of cracking.

Dan gave Matt a pat on the back before dropping him off at the trustee cottage, armed with the last bag of marijuana he'd have to smuggle inside.

"See you in eight days!" Matt turned and walked away with a rare smile he couldn't suppress.

Usually, the terms for leaving prison included having a place to live and a possible job. Without these stable factors and a support system, someone leaving the joint would be likely to return. Anyone without close friends or family had to go to a halfway house upon release. The board preferred that inmates have a job waiting as well, but they knew it was a challenge to line up a job from inside a prison, and besides, Matt would just go back to living with Dan and dealing drugs. He'd picked up schemes from other cons and had some ideas for adding to their drug trade.

Matt indicated on the prison exiting form that he'd look for a welding job once he got out. The man conducting the interview paused, shuffled through some papers—possibly those old IQ results—in Matt's extensive file, and gave a dissatisfied look. "Have you worked toward any degrees in prison? Have you considered getting a trade or enrolling in higher education?"

He did work toward a certification the second time in. Having a certification meant you could earn trustee status faster, so Matt chose the fastest course—welding. Though he gave another four years of his life to the prison, he got something else in return; a degree in running a successful drug trade. Each misstep took him closer to reaching a level where there would be no mistakes.

"I'm like one of those Hindus who keeps reincarnating until they reach perfection," he once joked with Dan, who replied that they should get him a cobra to charm out of a basket as well since Matt thought he'd never get bitten by the law.

Now he just had to coast through another week. He allowed himself to dream of freedom when motorcycles went racing past the trustee cottage. He had a friend up to the cottage for one last cookout, both a celebration and an unspoken thank-you for the letters he sent over the years. On winter days when Matt was cold, cooped up, and yearning to get his life back, sure enough, a letter from a friend would arrive. At this moment, he felt lighter, and a smile even crossed his face when one of the cool guards, a guy who didn't get off on enforcing every little rule, came to get Matt. But then he soured inside when the guard pulled out handcuffs and motioned for Matt to turn around.

"You're spending the night in Federal Hall," the guard said.

Matt's chest hammered so hard that it pulsed all the way up to his ears making the noise so loud it had to be audible to others, though he knew that wasn't possible. He concentrated on taking slow breaths and refused to let himself walk into the cell block looking whipped or worried.

"What's going on?" He asked it automatically knowing that no informative answer would follow. He spent a sleepless night convincing himself that whatever the charges were—it had to be the drugs, of course, but maybe it wasn't—they had no proof just as they were unable to figure out his "envelope-under-the-gap-scheme" a few months prior. They'd claim to have information, and he'd deny it. If drugs were involved, he reasoned, they'd have sent him to the hole. He didn't find out until the next day that all the holes were full; three of the lifers he supplied were filling those spots.

Snitch is not only a derogatory word inside prison but a dangerous one as well. Anyone christened with this unholy name risks impending death. The person who got ratted out would put a target on the snitch's back. Someone who was low on the hierarchy could rise in the ranks by hurting or killing a snitch, which meant the snitch was never safe. Through years of trial and error, the guys on the inside found a loophole for almost everything, including how to spot a snitch and knowing when a shakedown was going to occur. Matt was living in the trustee cottage, and where he no longer had to worry about a shakedown. On the inside, however, any forbidden item carried with it a consequence: for example, getting caught with prison hooch was an automatic thirty days in solitary.

The next morning a guard led him to a conference room containing nothing but a small table, two hard chairs, and a DCI agent who was hunched over a folder scanning through a page with his squatty forefinger as though his life depended on it. The man's appearance first struck Matt as mushroom-like, with puckery eyes that sank into an odd-shaped head void of hair. The man's paunchy midsection and tanned skin beneath a wrinkled polo shirt could have easily helped him pass for an elderly relative stopping by for a quick visit. He turned out to be all business though and introduced himself without fanfare, getting right to the facts. The first sentence hit Matt like a sucker punch since he was still, unrealistically he realized, hoping this wasn't really happening.

"Tell me about the marijuana you've been supplying to an inmate who works in the law library." The man's voice had that solid, confident tone that cops liked to use whether they are confident or not. Matt hedged his bet on the latter.

"I don't know anything about that," he replied with eyes that were just steady enough to indicate he wasn't trying too hard to look innocent.

"We have witnesses ready to testify that you have supplied at least four inmates with significant amounts of marijuana on multiple occasions." He flipped some pages and began reading off approximate dates and the amount of money that had exchanged hands.

"I don't know what you're talking about," Matt said, giving the standard con's denial and forcing himself not to shift in his seat. The more the man talked, the dimmer Matt's chances seemed. He put the pieces together and figured out there'd been a shakedown. None of the inmates had any warning, and several capfuls of pot were discovered hidden in a cell. In exchange for a lighter punishment, the inmates who got caught turned over the name of the mailman, who in turn gave up the names of the lifers. To avoid losing his job in the law library—"*it was like someone threatening to take my kid away, you know,*" Smiley later said—the lifers turned over the name of their supplier: Matt.

Eventually, there was a trial, and all of them took a plea after being presented with the snitches' written account and the bank statements among other damning evidence. The judge slapped three years onto Matt's sentence. The snitch went into protective custody and later requested to be transferred to a different prison. Smiley went in the hole for sixty days and lost his privileges to make phone calls, have rec time, or watch movies. He was especially distraught over not being able to use the phone since he rarely had visitors, and these calls were his only connection to

167

family on the outside. The mailman lost his job, but Smiley didn't. He coveted that job as much as life itself since there was nothing else to give him hope until the day he would breathe his last inside these walls.

The trip from the downtown courthouse to the prison passed in a surreal haze and hopes of riding his cycle faded along with the sun that had settled behind a cloud as though giving a warning. Now back in Federal Hall, the door clanked shut behind him, and after standing wordlessly for several minutes, he plodded over to the lower bunk where he sat listless as wet newspaper. Thus began the first of his additional 1,095 nights back in a cell containing a thin mattress and a CM with rancid breath who snored like a freight train. As he stared into the flickering shadows of the nighttime sidelights, a sickness washed through him over losing furlough and the bit of freedom he was able to taste as a trustee. Perhaps more than that, though he had never realized it until now, were the conversations with Dan. While Matt was more reserved and preferred observing over talking, Dan brought out the slice of extrovert in him, and now he probably wouldn't see him for years since Dan had yet to once visit him in prison.

Weeks later, when Mary came to visit as she did every two weeks, he complained to her that this God she wasted her time praying to didn't seem to be listening.

"You're the one not listening. I've been telling you for years to settle down." She met his eyes and didn't bother to soften her words.

"If you've been praying for me, why am I still here?" He dealt them each five cards and wondered how many hours they both wasted playing this game that neither one of them really enjoyed yet preferred over the uncomfortable silence. There was rarely anything new for Matt to talk about which resulted in awkwardly thin conversations. Mary spent her days working, reading, and going to church.

She met his eyes briefly. "You're here because you're breaking the law."

"Everyone breaks the law. You don't think none of them guards ever took bribes or the warden maybe used his position to get things no one else could based on who they are? Hell, cops are always on the take, and I don't see none of them in here." Matt tossed down a king of spades and drew the queen of hearts. It was against his better judgment, but he was a much better player than Mary and based on her transparent facial expressions he determined she was going for something unobtainable like a royal flush, hearts or diamonds. He was right. She bypassed the king and drew a new card, which she hovered midair as though it were a weapon she could use to halt the game 'til Matt came to his senses.

"But you *really* broke the law. God knows your heart isn't pure."

"So God is keeping me here?"

But Mary knew where this was heading and didn't take the bait. "He's given you a lot of chances, and you haven't reciprocated. Your being here *again* is proof enough of that." She waved a dismissive hand in a futile attempt to show she'd won that round.

He turned away abruptly at this remark as though the truth were a mirror and had reflected a piercing glint into his eyes.

"He's given me nothing, but tell the Big Guy to send me a blanket, so I don't have to keep freezing my a** off," Matt said, not able to look at Mary. There were still thousands of dollars in his bank account that would remain there because, for some reason, the court hadn't petitioned to get the money back. He refused to mention this and allow her to twist it, convinced it was a break that had nothing to do with God and everything to do with luck.

Chapter 33
The College of Crime

The tuition was steep. The professors were ruthless. The consequences of not paying attention were unforgiving. If you didn't learn a lesson correctly, it could cost you life or limb.

One of the teachers was "Murder Mike," a notorious biker gang member who had exterminated a rat during the Black Hills Sturgis Rally. Mike became aware that a federal informant had been planted into the gang to gather evidence on drug trafficking which could send him away for life. During the rally, Mike lured the federal informant to a secluded area outside of Sturgis. When the informant turned, the deadly stare on Mike's face gave away his intentions. Mike made the snitch get down on his knees and beg for his life. Despite this, the guy was shot in the head and tossed into a deep ravine.

His notoriety in prison paled in comparison to "The Enforcer," a hit man for a biker gang out of Texas. He didn't say much; with a closed mouth and cold eyes he conveyed what he wanted through looks alone, and no one messed with him. He'd gotten pinched in a drug setup along with assault, also at the Sturgis Rally, and was already a felon. In South Dakota, this translated into twenty-five years of hard time. When The Enforcer went up for parole for the first time, no one expected him to be successful. In this state, people with long stretches to serve did not get paroled the first time, especially when they were responsible for quietly creating havoc within the prison as he had done by culling a group of gang members. However, that turned out to be the very reason he was paroled on the first try. The state wanted to get rid of him and send him away before he caused more problems in the prison.

Always one to think ahead, Matt simply saw it as an opportunity to gain favor from someone he might do business with in the future.

Before The Enforcer left, Matt handed him a slip of paper with Dan's address on it.

"Stop by my brother's house before you leave town. I have a going away present for you." He'd arranged with Dan to have a large bag of marijuana ready. This show of respect could have paid off down the road, but Matt never had to use this card after all.

One day Matt was making deals with hired murderers and the next day improving his domestic skills. Lives on the inside were gridlocked—on pause, so-to-speak—so conversations centered around improving one's criminal exploits, getting back at someone, getting a setup, or previous sexual exploits. Sure there were occasional chats about family, but many cons didn't have much family worth discussing. So, they all ended up discussing the same old topics. Activities were stiflingly limited to gambling, playing cards, or watching TV. In winter, they didn't even get outside, though the razory Midwestern wind somehow found its way through the stone walls, supplying a steady flow of chilled air.

Matt's new CM cupped his hands and blew into them before pulling out a ball of yarn and two hooks. He started to crochet and watched undeterred for that look of dismay to cross Matt's face. When the CM noticed Matt's puzzlement, he decided to offer an explanation before the wisecracks started rolling in.

"It's better than sittin' like a couch potatah, and the time goes by faster."

Matt gave a slight nod. "That's right, Suzie." The cracks came automatically, especially when there had to be a less feminine way of passing time.

"It ain't hurting my parole app either cuz I'm showin' initiative."

Matt was never one for bow-tie grammar yet noted that the CM pronounced the last word more like *nishtiv*. By the end of the day, Matt had used up a skein of yarn and had to buy more at the craft store the next day. Sitting wasn't relaxing for him though. It never had been. Since shooting the breeze on a cycle wasn't currently an option, crocheting would have to do for the time being. He crocheted blankets and gave them as gifts for Christmas, having made Mary one with stripes. He gave it to her with the admonishment that she could wrap up on the couch and read those stupid, sappy novels of hers.

"Reading is harmless entertainment," she said a bit too somber.

Come to think of it, it was too bad that the two of them couldn't trade places. Mary would probably be just fine sitting in prison reading, watching TV, and talking all day. The only thing she'd miss would be the endless cups of coffee, and he couldn't picture her suitcasing hotwires even for that.

The slight embarrassment she caused him in handing over a bag of yarn and crochet hooks during these twice monthly visitations was outweighed by knowing the gift would provide some welcome relief from the grinding monotony. In fact, the bottomless pit of boredom had given rise to a virtual cottage industry within the prison, and the inmates supported each other with the same diligence as patrons of the arts. A cornucopia of arts and crafts sprung to life within the walls every day in the form of original paintings, woodworking, pottery, and metal crafts to name a few. At one point Matt traded a blanket and some commissary money for a phallically decorated marijuana bong disguised as a vase, which he gave to Dan for a Christmas present.

Chapter 34
Prison Ministry

Once a week, a van load of good-hearted souls from a local church paraded inside to bring the word of Jesus Christ to the prison heathens. The church members assembled in a room and any qualified prisoner who had no write-ups and wasn't in p.c. could join the group. Inmates had a few incentives for joining. Some craved the social interaction, others thought it would look good on their parole application, and a few were open to the idea of a personal savior who could forgive what many considered unforgivable crimes. Matt didn't fall into any of these categories.

"Come with me once, and see if you like it. It's some entertainment for an hour or so. Gets ya out of these same walls for a while." A scruffy, thin-faced guy with long teeth who was doing time for dealing drugs occasionally suggested this to Matt.

Matt referred to him as Weasel on the few occasions when he actually had reason to refer to him. "Nah, you can go sit with a bunch of people who think they're better than you. I'll stay here."

He'd never sat through an actual church service in his life yet recalled the hellish boredom of mass at Catholic school as something that would only appeal to those who considered waiting in line at the DMV or listening to classical music to be entertaining. He despised Weasel and most of the other inmates who attended the prison ministry. He considered them desperate sell-outs and didn't want to be associated with any of them.

"Okay, man. If you ever change your mind, you're welcome to join us."

Matt knew he would never change his mind. He'd never needed anyone to tell him what to do and had managed just fine so far. His mom, on the other hand, now attended church almost regularly and what did it get her? Two divorces, two messed up kids and a boatload of troubles. Even his nephew, Wade, had taken up with a wild crowd that drank too much, sold drugs, and broke the rules. Church was fine for people who needed arbitrary rules imposed on them. He had enough rules to follow without adding to the list, thank-you-very-much.

Mary was certain to be singing her same holy song today. She tried as much as possible to slip it into their normal conversation. When he appeared in the visitation room in blue jeans and an off-white T-shirt, Mary had already secured their favorite corner chairs and was leaned back with her head against the wall in a perfect position of patience. It was nothing more than a large room with hard chairs and tables, but it quickly filled to a crowd though the ruckus and noise around her seemed unable to penetrate the curtain of peace that graced her expression.

"I can't name one thing this God has ever done for me," Matt said to Mary once when she cornered him into listening to some church spiel.

Matt looked for signs, too. There were days on end in the pokey when he had nothing to do but think, and he was unable to come up with one event in his life where he could have credited some God with having any part of it.

"You see what you want to see. That's why. You're refusing to look at the fact that you being here is a miracle. You should be dead, you know that," Mary said, exhaling and tapping cigarette ash into an empty coffee cup.

"The reverse is true, too. You just see what you want. Something good happens, and you start claiming He's answered a prayer. Something bad happens, and suddenly it's God's will. Why

176

would it be His will for crap to happen to anyone if He's so powerful?"

"It's not like that." Mary shook her head and lit a cigarette. Matt had a way of stumping her.

She changed the topic. "You're the one who never wanted to be home. You were always running all over who-knows-where, friends showing up at all hours," she said with a wave of her hand, "racing around on those motorcycles. I'd think you'd clean up your act instead of wasting time here all cooped up."

Matt didn't waver. He'd gotten away with plenty, especially when the drug money had been good, and he was able to hire a lawyer who'd gotten him out of several charges. One charge was reduced to sixty days in the county jail to which he announced to his friends that he could do that much time standing on his head. But Mary had a point. His need for the fast life was unquenchable. Before coming here, he'd souped up a Mustang and raced it for time at Thunder Valley Drag Way in Marion, South Dakota, then painted 13.3 on the windshield, which indicated his fastest quarter-mile time.

"The only good thing, if you can call it that, about this place is I know what's gonna happen every day when I wake up. There aren't too many surprises here," he admitted. Until he said it out loud, even he hadn't realized that prison provided a certain predictability that was actually comforting. Later on, with nothing else to do, he briefly contemplated what Mary said. The thoughts lasted as long as any of his occasional good intentions. It seemed there was a mental gravity that pulled him back into the rough anytime he dared to think something that wasn't self-defeating.

177

Chapter 35
Pressure Cooker

Morale among the prisoners had diminished lately. The previous warden believed in giving prisoners some independence in order to encourage them to follow the rules as well as to promote rehabilitation by ensuring that the prisoners experienced making good decisions before being set loose. He rewarded compliant behavior and provided good food along with leniency in allowing numerous personal items in the cells. But there was new administration. Rules and regulations tightened. Posters were pulled down, rec time reduced, and the food, as a prisoner had so eloquently stated, now tasted like crap. All of this led tempers in the prison to heat up like a pressure cooker, which led to what happened in the spring of 1993.

The inmate population was angry about overcrowding. The air was stifling, and extra inmates meant extra heat added to already edgy temperaments. By midday, the cell was a furnace. The cement floor was only a few degrees cooler so that when he lay skin-to-floor the sweat evaporated, leaving Matt wondering if he were fusing with the dirt and iron of the prison. He longed for a piece of ice to rub across his chest or forehead so the melting water could run down the sides of his body in a chilling trickle, but the prison didn't contain so much as one cube. Not for the inmates anyway. Ice was a luxury in a place where everything was served lukewarm. The humidity never began to fade until dark, when it changed from suffocating to tolerable. Just enough to move from unbearable to miserable.

The prison population plodded through another winter of cold, breezy cells and chilly shower rooms to find spring had emerged in a change of seasons that failed to transfer inside the prison walls where everything remained stagnant. One day was just like the next. The few weeks of tolerable spring temperatures failed to ease the unrest that continued to bloom fungus-like throughout the cells.

Summer would soon bring with it the unbearably hot days that turned the cells into reeking saunas of bacteria. BO mixed with BMs from the open toilets in each cell, and during the muggiest days, the air became thick enough to wrap around his throat in an act of suffocation. Lacking a thermometer, he once estimated the temperature in the mid-90s with 90% humidity and no air flow. There were days he lay barebacked on the floor with a wet towel on his head trying to decide which was worse: the stifling heat of summer or the frigid winters when he could never seem to sleep comfortably from a lack of warmth. Now, mild spring weather brought forth a burst of spring outside and a burst of complaints inside.

"It's like the man is trying to drive us crazy," Matt's cellmate lamented before grabbing two fists full of cell door bars and trying to shake them, to no avail. There was something simmering within the iron pen; something almost tangible that left an unrecognizable taste in Matt's mouth. The inmates had few rights as it was, and some of those precious freedoms had been infringed upon. The Native American population had some of the most vocal grievances in wanting religious time for sweat lodges and the ability for personal leave to attend a Sun Dance for a vision quest. It was a lasting way for them to connect to their culture in order to bury addictions and violence and become spiritually active in their tribes to rehabilitate, but they were denied these vital ceremonies. The inmates felt the buzz of tension well before the prison staff realized the seriousness of what was considered endless griping. In the next cells, Matt heard voices rise among the clatter of daily prison life.

"Word is some of the guys here think it's time to protest."

"To who? You think anyone cares we're not happy here?"

But the strain couldn't be ignored. Warning signs flickered in the prison halls.

During the daily one hour of rec time, inmates could go out in the prison yard or go on the tiers outside of their cells. Matt decided to stay in the corridor and was playing cards when hostile shouts from the yard spilled inside the prison. A murmuring began close to the open doors and then raced through the tier. Someone yelled to the guard at the end of the corridor, and suddenly the doors between the prison and the yard slammed closed with a thud. The prisoners inside couldn't get out, but that also meant that the men in the yard couldn't get in. They were all trapped. Matt heard screams and shouts resonating outside but didn't know that about 200 inmates in the yard had gained control of the prison grounds and the buildings inside. It had begun with two inmates who were drinking homemade hooch and feeling overly confident as well as agitated. A fistfight broke out between them in the prison yard, and as more guards arrived to squelch the violence and haul the offenders to the hole, more inmates joined in until the guards were forced to pull back due to the number of injuries.

In Federal Hall, Matt rubbed his eyes that stung from the CS tear gas that was shot into the prison grounds, and the rancid smell of gas bled inside the cell block. He and his CM quietly discussed what was going on and if the rioters came in, who they might target for retaliation. Here they were trapped in their cells since the order had come down to lock up.

National Guard units and the police SWAT teams began arriving with automatic weapons that were aimed into the inmate-controlled grounds now clouded by smoldering chairs and other debris that had been set afire. Beneath billowing black smoke, the riot leaders brandished clubs, concealed their faces, and demanded to speak with negotiators. With the lives of the prison guards hanging in the lurch, some of whom had been beaten with weapons, this request was granted, and talks began. During the night, the inmates involved issued this request.

"One, freedom of religion. Two, investigation conducted into the State Department of Corrections concerning all staff members. Three, adequate health care." Then they demanded that these complaints be televised by the media.

By morning of the second day, the negotiators settled on an agreement that if the complaints were televised, they would then have to return to the prison one by one. And they did. Despite some serious injuries, no one died during the violent takeover. Parts of the prison were left in ruin. Three inmates were prosecuted, and the Department of Corrections changed several policies regarding inmate treatment. The state spent three million dollars on repairs and security upgrades.

Chapter 36
Back in the Groove.
Briefly.

The door widened to a hopeless sky that loomed dead and gray. The gate closed behind him, and Mary was waiting to drop him off at Dan's house again. Dan moved Matt in as though he were another box of nuts, bolts, and rusty wrenches. In the room where he now slept, Matt loaded up a box of chipped picture frames and cracked vases from a dresser drawer and smuggled them out to the garbage to make room for an underwear drawer.

"You find room to put your stuff?" Dan asked, then pointed to two additional cardboard boxes of clothes he'd been storing for almost three years.

Matt removed a busted lamp from the closet, which he waved in front of Dan. "You must buy glue by the gallon fixing up all that crap you keep in here," he said, hauling the contents of the boxes downstairs into a dusty light where he groped his way through a maze of plywood scraps, boxes of junk, and shelves bulging with deftly repaired household necessities in order to get to the washing machine. Each piece of clothing from the boxes shook forth a memory; boots Mary gave him for Christmas, but mostly T-shirts and jeans that he assumed were still in style, so they all went into one big load along with a capful of generic laundry soap. Mary came every Sunday to wash Dan's laundry and fill the refrigerator with leftovers for the week.

"Do you want goulash or spaghetti? I brought both," she yelled outside to Dan while unloading noodles and jars from grocery bags.

"Spaghetti," Dan answered impatiently, setting down his fourth beer of the afternoon and pausing to look up from a small engine he was fixing.

"What?"

"I said spaghetti!" Then he added half as loud, "You old bag."

"Spaghetti?" she shouted through the open window.

"Damn it! Get a hearing aid, woman!"

Charges piled up on Matt. In fact, the streets of the city seemed to have morphed overnight into a precarious maze of frustration with Matt as the rodent scurrying around to avoid getting caught in a dead end. He skirted the nightclubs since cops often moonlighted as bouncers there. The two DUIs he faced combined with the lack of a driver's license meant he had to drive slowly and carefully, yet no matter how much he intended to do this, the pedal ended up hitting the floor. Yesterday he was informed by the defense attorney that he might be charged as a habitual criminal due to his prior felonies, and this meant life in prison. He had no intention of ever returning to prison. There was only one solution to this crap life had dumped on him. He'd sell everything. Everything. He'd sell every possession that could be traced to him except a gun, take the money, and disappear into a big city. He'd never had to do it before, but he'd find a way to get an alias and eventually let Dan and Mary know where he was, but even then not until the trail leading to him was cold and dead. He needed a new identity; he'd become a different person.

The old Matt would cease to exist, and this carried with it the benefit of knowing that a big city wouldn't waste its time with petty charges the way this backwater state did.

Chapter 37
The Running Man

Yankton, South Dakota, a historic town woven along the Missouri River, is the Lake Tahoe of this sparsely populated corner of the state. Its lush parks, along with the shimmering blue water of Lewis & Clark Lake, attract both the down-to-earth fishermen and the upscale weekend boaters. Matt pulled into town intending to stay just long enough to unload some drugs to a friend of a friend who'd agreed to buy them. The heat was on, and he was preparing to step out of the kitchen just as soon as everything was in order.

"I'm going to need a lot more cash," he admitted to Dan after selling his favorite bike, a bright red Suzuki 1150cc.

"There's money to be made right here," Dan said distractedly, waving his hand over a mound of pot he was divvying into small plastic bags.

There wasn't time for that, and Matt knew his only option was to sell everything of value, except his .38 snub nose, and get out of town. Way out of town where no one would recognize him. His plan was to be gone that morning, but he wouldn't leave before making a trip to Sioux City, Iowa, to say goodbye to Phil, his old sidekick. Since Phil had changed his life, he didn't want Matt to come to his house while on the run, but their loyalty was unbreakable, so the two met in a dark parking lot instead.

185

"Bro, why don't you give me the gun before you split so there won't be a shootout," Phil said, appealing to Matt's logic.

"No way am I going down as a habitual criminal without a fight."

It was not what Phil hoped to hear. "Man, I love you like a brother. Those cops will kill you, or you'll kill some young cop with kids. Then they'll put the needle in your arm."

"That all may be, but I'd rather die in a shootout than go behind bars the rest of my life. And I'm keeping the gun. It's my insurance policy." They gave each other a parting hug, and Matt drove off into the night. Phil went home disheartened, thinking he'd never see Matt again.

After leaving Sioux City, he had one last stop in Yankton, South Dakota, to collect money someone owed him. Matt's mug shot had been distributed around the Midwest, and too many charges were pending, so he was anxious to leave. His foot instinctively reached out to floor the gas before he remembered he had to play it safe. He chugged up to a stop sign cursing the beat-up old truck he bought after losing his prized Mazda. He let a friend who was a known drug dealer drive it, the friend got pulled over, and the cops impounded the car even though they hadn't found anything illegal in it. Now Matt couldn't get it out of impound since he was wanted and was stuck with this blocky truck.

The Queen Anne and Colonial Revival homes on this quiet street cast exaggerated shadows across the windshield, and Matt took it as a good sign that he hadn't torn through the intersection like he might have on a typical day. A cop car rolled up to the four-way stop at the same time. *Can't catch Matt the Man this time, sucker.* But for some strange reason, the cop flipped on his lights.

"Damn!" He didn't hesitate or stop to wonder what triggered the cop's concern. He floored the gas and screeched around a corner to a straight-away. The truck bogged. It didn't shoot to top speed like the Mazda. Matt flinched. Speed was his ace, the edge that gave him the extra seconds he needed to perform his age-old magic trick of getting ahead of the cops before pulling into a hidden drive and killing the engine moments before the police car turned the corner and went whizzing past. He turned a corner, but the cop was right behind him. He tried it again and then once more, but he couldn't get any distance from this damn badge-beetle. Up ahead was an apartment complex with the potential for having a lot of tight turns. *Maybe he won't want to race where people could be walking, but I will.* He pushed the pedal hard and squealed into the driveway past a row of garage units then took the first turn, scanning for a hiding spot. The patrol car was right behind him. He turned another corner and swore before coming to a screeching stop. The truck lurched and threw Matt into the dash. He'd hit a dead end. He grasped around for his handgun, but it was nowhere to be found, apparently bouncing who-knows-where during the chase. With no time to spare, he threw the door open and bolted.

Sticks and leaves cracked beneath his pounding feet, and he slipped through loose dirt. After only a few minutes he was bent at the waist, straining to catch his breath, hiding deep in a ravine of trees. Living a party life didn't have him in shape for outrunning cops. Feeling like a hunted animal, he searched for a way out. There was a river, but it was too wide to cross, so he scanned for a path out of this wooded hiding spot that gave him the gift of cover. If he could get out of here and back into a neighborhood, he could find an open garage or backyard shed to hide in. He could hear the voice of the officer fading farther behind him with each stride. The cop called for backup though, and when the police eventually trapped him from all sides, he was finally knocked to the ground and handcuffed.

The empire he had so brazenly constructed on shifting sand crumbled after a series of small bumps which resulted in an unexpected domino effect. The jail's cell door clanked shut, and Matt soon had the seeds of a plan in place that occurred after he was served his first meal. His cellmate was a friend of someone with whom Matt dealt drugs, and his soft face gave him the appearance of a storybook rabbit. He was an edgy, soft-spoken fellow who looked at the floor when he talked, or rather mumbled. *Perfect.* The guy already knew Matt—that happened a lot when he ended up in jail—and the bunny man was too intimidated to cause trouble. He made a mental list of priorities, a sort of jailhouse triage. At the top of the list was avoiding trip number four to the state penitentiary.

"This jail might crumble apart in the next rain," Matt said, flicking crumbs of mortar from the window sill with the metal spoon he was given at supper. The inmates were expected to wash their utensils in the cell's sink and keep them for the next meal.

"Yeah."

"It's a damn old building, and the guards here don't seem all that wise either. Security is lax."

"Uh-huh." The little bunny of a man picked at his nails while Matt talked.

Matt dug his spoon into the groove of mortar between window and building and flicked the pieces in Bunny's direction, causing the man to throw his arms up in defense.

"Ever thought of blowing this place?" Matt hovered over Bunny, whose eyes were darting between the window and the crumbling cement that now lay scattered on the floor. He shrugged.

"Yeah, well, do whatever you want, but I'll be gone by the end of the week. You can come with me, or you can stay. Your choice." He checked the hallway for guards and cameras, found a container for the mortar crumbs, and went back to scraping the window.

Matt had almost broken his way around the window when a guard came and hauled him to solitary. The jail hole. Fearing he might get charged with aiding and abetting the escape, Bunny had ratted Matt out, and now there was nothing Matt could do but wait for his sentencing hearing. This time the charges were for more serious crimes, and his lawyer informed him he might be considered a habitual criminal.

The prosecutor was an unsmiling blowhard, who occasionally approached the judge at the bench in what Matt considered to be clearly covert attempts to railroad him straight into prison.

His disdain for Matt crystallized when he announced with no compassion, "This frequent visitor to the courts eluded the police and then attempted a daring escape from the county jail."

Daring? The accusation caught in Matt's throat. *The real crime here is the way these lawyers stretch the truth to their own advantage.* He knew the evidence was solid but also knew he couldn't stomach a long stretch in prison. He'd reached rock bottom but was seasoned enough to know that his opposition to being incarcerated would have no effect on the judge's decision. His only hope was in all that praying Mary did.

The trial was short, and the judge returned a verdict of ten years in the state penitentiary. Matt felt like someone had ripped his lungs out. And this time prison would be different. The terms of this sentence carried with it a condition that would nearly destroy his emotional balance, crush his spirit, and unhinge his sanity. Matt crumbled inside when he found out that based on his escape attempts and previous prison drug ring, he was sentenced to the penitentiary's hell-hallway.

Chapter 38
Ad Seg

" . . . four, five," he said to no one while performing an estimated heel-to-toe measurement of his cell, "six." He said the words again, yet they still seemed unreal. Was it possible to live in a cell six by nine feet wide for ten years, or possibly more since he still had charges to face in two other counties? His heart cinched. He'd only been there two hours and already felt clammy. He put one hand over his rapidly beating heart and then walked over to the toilet and the cracked sink, rubbing one hand across the distorted metal mirror, before lying down on the mattress. Some protective mechanism prevented his brain from contemplating ten more years in this solitary cage, locked up like an animal who couldn't be trusted to interact with prisoners in the general population. Ten years was 120 months or 3,650 days. With almost no human contact. The saying *time marches on* never met a prison. Matt was shoved in a cell and cryogenically frozen in time. By night, he was overcome with sweaty trembles. Anxiety squeezed his throat, and he pulled at the covers, feeling as though someone had wrapped chains around his windpipe, which didn't seem like a half bad idea. It had been less than a day, and he was already shaking uncontrollably. His only view was of pale-gray block walls moist with condensation and a gray steel door that contained only two openings, one a small window and the other a thin rectangle which allowed a food tray to be passed through. This was also where Matt would be ordered to stand and turn around with his hands behind his back in order to be handcuffed before being moved from the cell. The solidness of the door had the effect of making a small space seem torturously confining.

Prison authorities deemed him a security risk and a threat to the operations of the prison system due to his past drug operation inside the facility and the near jail-break in Yankton. In light of this, he was assigned to the Administrative Segregation wing. Ad seg. The words struck fear among inmates; most would do anything to avoid the mental anguish of this psychologically troubling wing of the prison. It was isolated from the rest of the prison, a circular two-story tier built around a main control pod where the guards worked. The inmates spent twenty-three hours isolated in their cells every day. The only view of the outside was through a small window with a view of an unused part of the prison yard.

He left for one hour each afternoon. With shackled hands and feet, he was led to one of two 8 x 20-foot cages for "exercise," then to a locked shower stall, and all of this could take no more than sixty minutes. In winter inmates from ad seg were taken to an open, empty area of the prison instead where they could move around and get a view of different institutionally dull walls. This brief escape from the crushing confines of a cell gave just enough relief to Matt, who was teetering between sanity and the unknown. At night he felt the silence clutching at all of the untapped possibilities he'd never experienced due to wasting his life behind bars.

The inmates who'd been here for years had devised ingenious ways to create entertainment and pass the time. They used squares of toilet paper to create models of airplanes and other origami figures. Toothpaste was molded like clay to make figures of people, animals, or rooks and pawns to use for solitary games of chess. Matt tried to think of any angle to give himself hope. Occasionally prisoners from the general population were sent here for long stretches if they threatened or attacked a guard or habitually were sent to the hole. These prisoners were allowed a roommate but only if two people were in for a long time and hadn't received a death sentence. He held out hope that someday he might at least have this human contact. Until then he read, did push-ups, and tried not to go cabin crazy. Dan wrote to him and asked if he was going buggy being by himself all day. *Nah, I got a couple demons living with me,* Matt was tempted to reply, but this misery was something he had to bear on his own.

The dehumanization was of little concern to the prison staff. Matt knew he was here as punishment for the drug ring he organized his last trip in rather than for the seriousness of his crime. And if the other inmates went a little crazier before getting a final needle in the arm, it was just the price to pay. These degenerates, slouching in their cells, the lowest society could scrape up, were Matt's only company and even then only sporadically. There wasn't much to talk about since they all did the same thing every day. Nothing. So, they talked about their favorite sports teams and rehashed old Super Bowl games. It was a motley selection of company to choose from. Still, whatever human interaction he could garner, he exploited to the fullest. His sanity depended on his tier mates in spite of the fact that they had no sanity themselves.

Chapter 39
Meet the Neighbors!

Each section of ad seg was painted a different color, and Matt's section was painted shit-brown. Reluctantly, he came to know the others in this depraved, forgotten corner of the prison. Most of the time, he was the only one without a death sentence hanging over his head. Bit by bit, his tier mates' stories came out and only then after being filtered through a psychopathic lens. It wasn't until years later that he learned the real stories behind the hardened faces.

Donald Moeller

Donald grew up in an impoverished neighborhood north of Sioux Falls and was considered to be deeply disturbed as a child. His stepfather and mother traveled with the carnival and would leave him tethered to a rope at night so they could go about town partying. His mother despised him, called him a bastard, beat him senseless at times, and performed sex acts with men she met at the bar in front of her children and stepchildren. Christmas and birthdays were never celebrated in his house. By age eight, he regularly drank himself to sleep.

"Donald was a few years older than me, and here he was a twelve-year-old kid just sitting up in a tree all day long with a blank look on his face. Unless he noticed you walking by. Then his eyes turned cold like they were filled with hate," Matt's friend Phil said. As a child, Phil coincidentally lived a few doors down from Donald just as Matt did now.

195

He began his reign of terror as a teenager, often attacking people with bicycle chains or clubs. He was arrested for several sexual assaults including one in which he tied up a thirteen-year-old boy, forcing him to perform oral sex at knifepoint. As a child, he began serving time. In between incarcerations, he abducted nine-year-old Becky O'Connell off the streets of Sioux Falls while she was walking between her home and a nearby grocery store to buy sugar to make lemonade. He drove her to a secluded area east of town, then raped and sodomized the little girl while repeatedly stabbing her. Some of the stab wounds were so deep they went up to the handle of the knife. He then slit her throat. A sheriff described it as the worst thing he'd ever seen.

Moeller didn't talk to anyone, and no one talked to him. Prior to moving to this new ad seg wing, there was a covering across much of his cell door to prevent the other prisoners from throwing things at him. Among the hardened criminals in ad seg, Donald was at the bottom of the heap. It was another fifteen years before Donald was put to death but not before finally admitting, "If the rape and murder of Rebecca O'Connell does not deserve the death penalty, then I guess nothing does." Following his execution, cheers arose throughout the prison.

Robert LeRoy Anderson

Larisa Dumansky discovered her car tire was flat when she left work early one morning, unaware that it was intentionally deflated. Robert Anderson appeared almost immediately to offer her assistance. Dumansky was never seen alive again.

Piper Streyle was at home with her young children on the acreage she and her husband owned. When Piper failed to show up for her job, a co-worker phoned to find out where she was. Streyle's three-year-old daughter answered and said, "I don't want my mommy to die. She is probably killed." Her body was never found; however, the Sioux Falls detectives still solved the cases. Anderson had painted his SUV with washable black paint that he was able to wash off following the abductions. His vehicle had been fitted with a special board on which each corner had eye rings and chains so the women could be shackled spread-eagle to accommodate

Anderson's sexual inflictions before he slowly suffocated them. Anderson was eventually caught and sentenced to death in March of 2003. He was later found hanging in his cell from a noose he'd fashioned from a bed sheet.

Charles Rhines "The Donut Man"

Rhines went to the Dig 'Em Donut Shop in Rapid City to rob the store where he was previously employed. Donnivan Schaeffer, a courier, came upon Rhines rummaging through the office. Rhines came at Schaeffer, stabbing him twice with a hunting knife. Schaeffer begged Rhines to call an ambulance. The heartless man repeatedly stabbed Schaeffer to death, leaving the shop smeared with pools of blood, before walking away with $300. In Rhines's confession, the Rapid City Police Chief recalled that Rhines talked calmly before bursting out with an awful laugh much louder than his normal voice. The cold, haunting confession moved the jury.

His prior convictions along with this murder resulted in a death sentence. Rhines protested his sentence, explaining, "It's not like it was a major crime."

Elijah Page

Nineteen-year-old Chester Poage just wanted friends but made the fatal mistake of befriending Elijah Page. One cold March day, Page and two accomplices drove Poage to a secluded, wooded area near a mountain stream and then kicked him in the head over thirty times, stabbed him in the neck, pummeled him with large rocks, and made him beg for his life, torturing him for over three hours. Then they forced the man to strip naked and get into the icy stream. Still unsatisfied, they forced Poage to drink acid. His body wasn't found for weeks. Prior to his execution six years later, Page was asked if he had any last words.

"No," he said.

"Did you understand the question?"

"Yes. No last words," he said again.

Matt's photo from when he entered the Ad-seg wing where he was placed due to being a security risk to the prison. He was housed there along with death row inmates and prisoners who were extreme discipline problems.

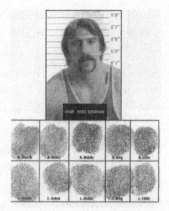

Co-author Phil Hamman's mug shot and fingerprints for a serious assault charge—one of several arrests during the time he and Matt ran the streets.

Chapter 40
Misery

Months of languishing next to society's most evil in a vile cell block led to depression. The loneliness materialized into physical pain. The only break from this despondency was the occasional infusion of more dysfunction. Someone screaming in his cell all day or a few days spent trying to convince the prison staff that there was an urgent medical need that required a visit to the infirmary. There was more excitement in the hole where inmates on the brink of madness would belligerently refuse to return a food tray or even throw feces. And when that excitement ceased, the others slumped onto their thin mattresses, as disheartened as the day after Christmas and knowing there probably wouldn't be another conflict for ages. In ad seg, however, the cycle of boredom slugged along. Through necessity, Matt found a way out of prison by escaping within his own mind, a mind superior to others in its ability to connive, manipulative, and survive. He closed his eyes, lay back, and summoned the feeling of an outdoor breeze until he could feel the wind on his face, fresh air blowing over his body, and his T-shirt rippling while flying down a sunny stretch of highway on a motorcycle. Another day he hiked a path through pine trees and along crystalline mountain lakes with their snow-capped peaks beckoning in the distance. There were always nice-looking women, and the sex was good. In between bits of reading and push-ups, his mind writhed in pain. He sometimes awoke in a panic and was taken aback by the fear that cinched its bulging arms around his chest making each breath unbearable.

Inside the control center, a prison guard sat with his chair tilted back. The cell block grew increasingly warmer, and over the years Matt learned to take advantage of any relief from the smothering summer heat; he leaned his head against the cool sink or lay nearly naked on the cell floor to absorb the slight coolness that formed when sweat from his body met the warm cement floor and evaporated. There was little air circulation, and with the high temperatures and humidity, the cell became a sweltering sauna. This was when the claustrophobia set in like a fiery demon in the heat of summer to torture the last remaining shreds of his sanity. He came to realize that the thick air wouldn't actually drown him by the day's end, it would only make the hours between more unbearable than usual. Strangely, though, there seemed to be visible heat waves radiating from the guard's badge, belt buckle, even the words from his mouth which Matt couldn't quite make out.

His existence no longer mattered. It was as if he'd ceased to exist and now was only taking up space like a box put into storage and forgotten. *They're here to melt me. I'll evaporate, fuse with the walls, and become part of this prison forever.* Then for a brief moment, he realized the thought was preposterous. *I'll ask the waitress for a glass of water.* He knew then that everything would be okay. He just needed a cold drink. He lay back on the warm bed, but even this wasn't a relief from the frightening anxiety the heat had branded upon his brain. The mattress enveloped him like a giant heating pad. He yelled at the waitress to hurry up with that ice water and then fell asleep.

But imagination can only do so much for a withering soul in need of a more nutritious source. There was an ever-present feeling that time had stopped. Was he going crazy? Shadows shifted, the room darkened, and a chill announcing the arrival of winter entered the air. Another meaningless day had passed, and without meaning, it was as if the day never really existed at all. The reality of a wasted life was becoming too bitter to accept. He went through his exercise routine of push-ups and sit-ups for the sixth time. Then from seemingly nowhere he began imagining Mary's voice talking about God. *If he cares about the birds and beasts and made each one by hand, imagine how much he cares about you. And I care about you too! You know that, and I'll never give up on you. God can work wonders in your life. Miracles even!* "Bull****," he hissed. If there was a God, this had been His big chance to give out a miracle and get Matt the hell out of here, but clearly, He'd blown it.

Even a shadow of hope would have stopped the ugly idea from germinating. Despair had sunk him so deeply into a hole that not even light could penetrate the black walls of his core. And the only shadows here were the ones that filled the corners and hidden places with gloom. But then something happened. Something much bigger than Matt, who had hours to daydream and contemplate, could ever have imagined. This life-changing event carried with it a hidden seed, of the mustard variety obviously, that would propel his life out of the gutter once and for all. The ability for him to eventually see this gift for what it was had perhaps been driven into his soul with shouts of *"Amen"* at Catholic school or inhaled from a heartfelt *"Welcome"* while walking through church on the way to steal the newspapers from the church steps.

It wasn't working. Closed-eye visions of beautiful mountains, blue seas, or the fast life became bad reruns and no longer gave even a few minutes of relief from the stifling boredom that pressed like a suffocating hand over his thoughts, his sanity. Loneliness made for an ugly enemy who never left his side. The absence of meaningful human contact meant that every movement he made was judged only by the shadows and gloom. Matt pressed his head against the cold steel bars and looked with disgust upon the derelicts that lined the opposite side of the cell block and wondered what he was doing among them.

Further down the corridor, howling sobs transitioned to a chortle and then manic laughter before turning back into howling sobs. Crazy sounds. Panicked, he clutched his chest. *Am I hearing the noises in my head? Am I the one howling?* He pinched his skin. That's what everyone says to do to make sure you're awake. He was. Or was he? Maybe he only imagined the pinch the way he imagined walks through the mountains. Nothing seemed real. Everything seemed painful. It was the first ring of hell, and the heat was still unbearable. Maybe it was time to end it all. There were no shoelaces, belts, or other convenient hanging materials allowed in here, but there were blankets that could be torn into strips, and there was only a minimal night crew to keep tabs on everyone. Death seemed preferable to this agony of loneliness and psychological torment.

To extinguish the thought, he got up, splashed his face with water that trickled from the sink. He cupped his hand beneath the faucet, watching the water overflow from his palm. The clear water reminded him of something, tapped into a distant memory. What was it about the water that seemed so hopeful? He walked to the cell door, then to his bed, and back to the sink, aimlessly, before sinking back on the bed and closing his eyes. He ate, exercised, did push-ups on the floor, and read a book, although he couldn't concentrate. Something unseen was pulling at the edges of his mind, prodding him. He tried to ignore it and lay back on the bed, where he began the process of imagining the wind, feeling the breeze, but somehow thoughts of his mom and nephew wandered in from nowhere like mental photobombers.

Every ninety days, inmates in ad seg were given a review and a brief psychiatric evaluation. Now Matt sat, hands cuffed, in front of a review board while they inspected his file and peppered him with questions. He'd had perfect behavior and no write-ups in the last three months.

"What kind of behavior do you expect we'd see from you if you were returned to the general population?" The counselor seemed genuinely concerned about Matt's answer, and this alone gave him hope.

"I'd follow the rules of the prison and continue to not get any write-ups."

"Would you try to escape again?" the head of security asked.

"No. I'm prepared to pay my debt to society."

"What would you do to demonstrate rehabilitation?"

Matt turned to the deputy warden who'd asked the question and answered with the response he'd been practicing for the past week. "I intend to take advantage of advanced welding courses and pursue other technical courses that would equip me to gain meaningful employment once I'm released."

The group murmured among themselves for a few minutes while Matt pondered whether there were any opportunities for escape in this room should he ever return here.

"I don't believe you belong here." The counselor spoke first, and the others nodded in agreement.

*Damn right I don't belong here. You f****** put me here as revenge for running a drug ring out of the prison and embarrassing the higher-ups.*

Before Matt had time to contemplate more convincing answers, he was removed from ad seg and put into the general population with a new CM, a guy Matt recognized from some jail time years ago. Having expected to serve out his time in ad seg, being put in the general prison felt like freedom. The human contact and television set were more welcome than any gift he could ever recall receiving. A few weeks later, though, a guard escorted him to a conference room. His heart somersaulted. *They're bringing me back to ad seg.* Although he'd done nothing wrong, he hadn't yet acclimated to the new freedoms and sometimes woke up with a jolt, unsure of where he was or even what year it was. Being incarcerated felt like a time warp; life on the inside was at a standstill, but life on the outside rushed along without him.

Eventually, the head of security showed up with a file and spilled the news. The same rat who'd turned him in as an escape risk back in the Yankton jail had gotten himself pinched again. In an effort to reduce his sentence, he'd fabricated a story about claiming to know that Matt had an elaborate plan to escape from prison. Eventually, the rat's story unraveled as fiction but not before causing Matt a couple of sleepless nights.

Chapter 41
Soul Searching

And then over the course of a year, a chain of events unfolded so miraculously that Matt could no longer deny that there was something more powerful at work. It started with his nephew getting booted from his collegiate wrestling team in South Dakota following a violent fight.

Hours later Dan breathed a sigh of relief when Wade showed up at the house, though he smelled of alcohol and looked wrung out.

"What *did* you do, boy?" Dan was more flabbergasted than angry. The end of the street had been full of cop cars earlier, and some sat for hours before leaving.

Wade had been at a college dorm party that night drinking beer with his wrestling buddies when one of them shoved someone through a window, which eventually led to a violent fight as well as Wade beating up a campus cop. Wade had the idea to weave their way an hour back to Sioux Falls hoping that time would allow the whole thing to blow over.

"We were at Renschler's Truck Stop rehashing what happened and talking too loud, I guess, because there was a cop sitting in a booth who overheard us talking about what happened. We were so stupid drunk at the time, we just didn't care."

"Yep. Never there when you need one, but always there when you don't," Dan interjected.

"When I walked past the cop, he stood up and put my hands behind my back. Then he started escorting me outside. I rolled my wrists, got away, and starting hitting him until he fell backward. He screamed, *Why are you striking me? I'm a Sioux Falls police officer!*" Wade, still unsteady on his feet, pulled a chair out from the kitchen table and stumbled into it. "I took off sprinting, and he pulled his gun out and yelled for me to freeze, but I ran nonstop over three and a half miles from Renschler's all the way here!"

"Those stupid f******!" Dan said, throwing his hands into the air. "Those cops'll kill someone one of these days pulling out a gun like they're in some movie just for a kid being in a fight."

Wade had to leave and wrestle at a junior college in Minnesota after his legal problems caused him to get barred from all of the state's colleges.

Then the call came from Wade's lawyer: "You're being charged for the assault on the Sioux Falls police officer."

Wade's heart sunk. This put a halt to his athletic dreams and his goal of becoming a doctor. He left college assuming he would serve time for the felony. Amazingly, though, the paperwork and charges disappeared. A friend with connections in the court records did some checking and reported that there was no trace of the arrest warrants.

"Now *that* is a miracle," Mary crowed on her next visit before presenting Matt with a bag of yarn.

"I hope he takes advantage of it and doesn't just get in more trouble." Matt realized the irony in this and considered that he should have taken his own advice years ago.

"He is. He already enrolled in another college and is going to take some *pre-doctorate* classes." She said this with such pride that it made Matt wonder what it would feel like to have someone talk that way about him.

"He's always been smart. He'll do good if he stays out of trouble."

"Believe me, I've been praying about that."

Matt was going to let the comment slide after having been on the non-receiving end of her prayers for years. "You know, if there was even a shred of proof that God existed I'd be the first believer. It sounds like a bunch of made-up crap to me."

"A shred of proof?" Mary leaned forward in disbelief. "There are so many shreds all *over* the place that you've got a pile of confetti at your feet! You're waiting for some big miracle, and not everyone gets that in life. You have to look for the little things: the miracle of life, the sun rising in the morning, and all that stuff. Life is a one-time offer, Matt, and you're spending it thumbing your nose at the One who created you."

Matt wasn't sure if she meant herself or God. Sometimes there was no arguing with her irrational reasoning. Maybe for him, nothing less than a miracle could balance out all of the crap. If God wasn't afraid to let him suffer at the hands of so many people, then He shouldn't hesitate to throw out a miracle here or there either. Mary and Matt locked eyes, and he got the distinct feeling that she was silently praying for a miracle in spite of his resistance.

After serving a few more months of his sentence, Matt was presented with a brief trip outside the walls, but the backhanded blow to this was that it was to appear in court. When he'd first arrived here, it was after being sentenced to ten years. Those weren't the only charges he faced, however, so today he was shackled and taken to the Minnehaha County court to face assault and drug-related charges as well as parole violations. The sweltering July air held promise; perhaps it was unspoken wishes from his birthday a few days ago that generally went unmentioned. He'd turned thirty-eight and on the way to the courthouse tried to figure out how many birthdays he'd spent behind bars; maybe fourteen, but it was hard to remember. At the courthouse, he met briefly with his lawyer, a man he'd met only once before. He'd beaten a lot of charges in the past, and maybe the judge would be in a good mood today. Thoughts of cases he'd lost pulled at the edges of his brain though.

While the prosecutor laid out evidence and called witnesses, hopes of beating the charges faltered, but he remained unrattled.

207

Unease and anguish had washed over him in ad seg that never completely left. The nightmares were not only more frequent now but also left remnants of twisted memories that nagged his conscience throughout the day making it seem as though the bad dreams never stopped. His own lawyer's words sounded hollow. *Under the influence. Assault. Battery. Remorseful.* More than likely he was thinking Matt couldn't possibly beat the charges and was only hoping to get the lightest sentence possible. When the trial finally ended, the judge slapped an additional thirteen years onto his sentence. It would be served concurrently with his ten years, but it still meant additional years added to his sentence. His sanity had been held in balance by the wisp of hope that had hung on beating this rap. Mary's words came back to him. *Your being here is a miracle. God is watching out for you!*

"This is crap," he said to no one in particular on the way back to prison. What kind of God lets someone suffer like this? The worst wasn't over. The most serious charges of all were still waiting for him in a drug trial in another county that should be coming up any week now. He was just waiting to hear that the paperwork had come through. The evidence against him was overwhelming and when added to today's sentence could potentially mean he'd still have decades to serve behind bars. In spite of the seriousness, the lawyer representing him hadn't yet bothered to arrange a meeting.

"All them judges and lawyers stick together. It's a big scam," his CM later commented upon hearing about the thirteen years.

"Yeah, this lawyer today didn't seem too interested in helping me beat this rap. No matter what happens to me, he still gets to go home to his family at night."

Then another serendipitous event occurred. Months passed with no word about the additional charges. *Just wait*, everyone told him. Charges don't just disappear. It hadn't happened to anyone, and one evening the whole tier buzzed with theories about the missing paperwork because such a thing hadn't happened to any of them throughout their numerous encounters with the law. *Just when you let yourself get convinced that there's been a miracle, here will come those charges and hit you like a bull*, the other inmates repeatedly reminded him with a bit of self-satisfied glee. But then years passed, and the paperwork for the expected twenty-year sentence never arrived at the prison. Ever.

God knows I've had enough. I can't take anymore. And as soon as he thought it, he immediately began wondering what had caused him to credit God for anything.

"I think I did get my miracle," he said to himself aloud, feeling that God must have known he'd had enough, and the lost paperwork was a sign that was stronger than a coincidence. He regretted having allowed his life to get swallowed up in the shadows of evil. The same thought reappeared in his head over and over. *God knows I've had enough. He's giving me my big break.* But he didn't voice this to anyone. He buried this seed of a thought deep inside his subconscious to germinate. Still, every day a little thought would push itself to the front of his brain. *Why are you here? Where should you be?* He didn't know where the two thoughts had come from. He sifted through a dung heap of memories that had been festering in his brain the last few days. How the hell had life brought him here? What had gone so wrong? Wade was on the right track now, good thing since the odds were stacked against him just as they'd been for Matt. Phil, his buddy, had made a good life for himself too, went to college, became a teacher, and had a family. *Why not me?* Matt whispered as though confiding in an invisible friend. His head flicked to see if anyone had noticed him talking to himself, but of course, no one had. Why was he still festering in this hellish sewer? But over the days and weeks to come, the thoughts became more powerful and vivid in his mind. He was helpless to control them. *God finds a way when there seems to be no way,* someone once said to him.

Chapter 42
Metanoia

Matt woke up to stillness and eerie silence and had the unsettling sensation that everyone had disappeared. He sat up, then adjusted to the sounds that had always been present but were somehow buffered by a peace that had settled over him during the night and tamped the usual chaotic buzzing of thoughts that cluttered his mind. For the first time, Mary's impending visit today created an odd eagerness in Matt. There were some ideas he wanted to hash over with her, but they didn't have the type of relationship that led to discussions about the meaning of life or philosophical ideas. So when she showed up, right on time as always, he stuck to the usual routine of asking how everyone was doing, especially Wade. He was proud of his nephew and thankful that he no longer shouldered any blame for being a bad influence on the boy.

Mary's face lit up at the mention of Wade. She had so little to be proud of, and Matt knew this, though it was the first time he'd ever felt pity for the woman who'd endured so much pain yet delighted in any bit of joy that came her way. "He's on the honor roll! He's *so* smart." Then a hint of despair registered in her eyes. "Like you." The words hung uncomfortably in the air saying more than two words should be expected to convey: *You're smart, and you could have gone to college. This should have been you, too.*

The urge to agree overcame him, but for now, it was enough to him that he was at least entertaining the thought that maybe it still could be him. Well, he was too damn old for college, but there was a lot he could do that didn't involve rotting in a cell. *It still could be me.* He shook the thought from his head and dealt them each five cards. For all his faults, Matt was observant. He'd been learning from the best since the days of Henry and Spike.

"I heard he got all religious, too." He took a long swig of his soda to quench a suddenly dry throat. "You gotta be happy about that. He turned his life around."

Mary nodded, and the edges of her mouth softened. How did she manage to say so much without uttering a word? He noticed a peacefulness in her eyes and a hint of joy in the way her mouth turned up. Her happiness touched him in a novel way. Here he was, all these years later and still figuring out how to scam his way through life even though he was minus nineteen years of his life he'd handed over to the penal system as an extra kick in the face. Suddenly he realized that it had been a burden to Mary as well.

A mother's love is strong. Relentless. On the outside of the prison walls, Mary had prayed continuously for her family. She considered it a miracle that Wade ended up on the right track considering his unstable childhood. Friends had prayed, and the power in these prayers had banded together to fill Matt with the tingling sensation of peace. God moves in mysterious ways, and this wisp of peace felt strange yet uplifting after a life of violence and crime. Images of people he respected flitted into his thoughts. *What do these successful people have in common?*

It was a holiday, they all ran together, and the visitation room was filled with moms both joyous and despondent. A thin, anxious woman with blonde hair pulled into a ponytail struggled to keep her balance while two preschoolers hugged her legs. She thrust a wide-eyed little boy into the arms of an inmate with a cheerful, "Tell Daddy how much we've missed him!" at which point the toddler burst into tears at the sight of this stranger. For some, their loved ones lived 360 miles on the other side of this state, making visits difficult and costly.

Mary had already had a lunchtime celebration with Dan and now entered looking as though she'd sprinted here, breathless but beaming and not waiting to sit down before announcing, as though the whole sentence was one word, "Wade was baptized in water and spirit today! He has a new life!"

Matt stroked his chin reflexively. "Oh, yeah?" He wasn't completely surprised. Letters from his nephew had been arriving more frequently.

Dear Uncle Matthew,

I miss our philosophical talks. I think this tendency to analyze, or perhaps overanalyze life is something I inherited from you, and for that I am grateful. I was dissecting a cadaver this week in medical school when a thought crept into my mind. The nervous system controls the body, but what controls the nervous system? Cadavers have a nervous system, but they can't move. Where did their life go? What change occurred that caused them to go from walking, talking, laughing humans to this? How would you answer that?

A few weeks later he received this one.

Dear Uncle Matthew,

You'll like this story! Some big guy in my chemistry class keeps inviting me over to his place to study. The dude weighs at least 275 pounds and is super nice to me for some reason. He wouldn't stop asking me to stop over, so finally, I went with a friend because I suspected he was coming on to me. When I got to his apartment, he cornered me and said, "You HAVE to accept Jesus now!" He gave me a Bible and told me that once you commit to follow Christ, it is worse to turn away from Him than to never have served him. It made me kind of nervous. I wasn't ready for that, but I took the Bible. When my friend and I left, we had a good laugh, but I have to tell you that

> *something he said stuck with me. Maybe it's like the verse*
> *in Corinthians—maybe he planted a seed in me.*

A seed. Maybe that explained it. For the first time it made sense. The forced isolation brought him to contemplate why some people close to him were on the right track. He couldn't deny that he'd felt small tremors of some mysterious force that seemed to be shaking the selfishness right out of him. The urge to swindle his way through life started fading. For decades he'd lumbered through life, blind to all he'd been missing. Now, something moved him. Changed him. He opened his mind to the idea of allowing himself to be transformed from a law-breaking heathen into someone he was supposed to have been all along. While he'd been plummeting down a rocky cliff, head first, God had been waiting to catch him and set him upright again.

Chapter 43
Altered

Six and a half years later, the steel gates opened for Matt, and he walked out. With good time and no write-ups, he was paroled. It was an anticlimactic moment. One minute he was a prisoner, the next a free man. In the movies, the long-suffering girlfriend waits in the parking lot, surprising the ex-con with her dedication, celebratory music plays in the background, and the sun shines over the horizon. For Matt, the unexpected ending was that he would not be returning to a life of crime. His old life receded in a series of turns and twists down new roads. He'd spent nineteen of his forty-four years locked away from society. He'd celebrated at least eighteen birthdays behind bars. Mary was there to pick him up at the gate. Dan had a room waiting for him. Same song and dance on the outside, but on the inside, there was a lot of editing going on. He hadn't changed completely. On the outside, he was the same, but he'd taken the insides down to the studs and was ready to rebuild.

He'd been out a week when a former cellmate called.

"Hey, I haven't seen you since hard rock lockup three years ago." It didn't take long for this former friend to get down to business. "I got an inside line on a score that will be easy cash, but I need a partner."

Matt cut him off. "I got a new life and don't want any part of this. Don't call again." Hanging up the phone felt as though he'd placed the proverbial final nail in the coffin that buried his criminal past.

It's said that God comes to those in their darkest hour when people are at their lowest point. Matt essentially cut ties with his old life and started over in a place where nearly everything was new and unfamiliar. This same fear of an unknown God and the thought of being confined by someone else's rules that had once kept him at arm's length from faith now brought him to his knees. He had nothing to tether his existence and grasped at a silent yet substantial notion that he was doing the right thing. At that point Matt had a sudden urge to read the Bible; it seemed to be his only lifeline. He pulled it from the drawer, a gift from Mary, where it had waited patiently for its cover to be lifted so the words could spill forth. She had marked a verse: *So we do not lose heart. Though our outer self is wasting away, our inner self is being renewed day by day. 2 Corinthians 4:16.* He felt God telling him it was time to change. Then there was the strong feeling that things were about to fall into place.

He got another unexpected phone call. This time it was from his daughter. Over the next months, they worked to build a relationship out of nothing.

Knowing that it had been years since Matt had spent time with a woman, Wade decided to bring Matt to a gathering and introduced him to Pam, the mother of his best friend. Pam was tall and attractive in a way that can only happen when the beauty starts from the inside and works its way to the surface of the skin. Wade then headed out on purpose, leaving Matt with no ride home. It worked. Matt and Pam connected.

Matt had started changing his ways. It had been more difficult to re-assimilate into a normal routine after such a long sentence. He'd started working an honest job making deliveries. He no longer had any desire to go to parties or bars. He wasn't sure where he fit now, so he spent a lot of time at Dan's. When Pam showed up, the two fell into easy conversations that led into the wee hours of the night.

Pam grew up in Yankton, South Dakota, the same town where Matt was arrested. She'd grown up in a typical middle-class family with a brother and sister. Her mom was a teacher and her dad worked for the government. Pam savored life and relished peace and harmony. The tranquility Matt felt around her stirred him. All along he'd been searching out the adventure and frenzied emotions he credited for fueling his zest for life; had these things in fact been masking an inner compass seeking peace? They were a mismatched set, no doubt, yet opposites attract, and something kept pulling them together.

"You're a good person," she said, unaware that for Matt the fleeting words hung weighted in the air as if tethered by invisible ropes. For most people, this phrase would have gone almost unnoticed, but for Matt, it was a first. When *was* the last time someone had referred to him as good? In the warmth of her smile, he trembled, and his heart raced.

"Are you okay?" she finally asked, putting a tender hand on his forearm. Pam had noticed that the readjustment back into society, along with making drastic changes in his life, was still challenging Matt. For weeks their relationship didn't move beyond watching TV, including vintage Billy Graham crusades. No one could deny the positive effect of Pam's goodness on Matt. Without any prodding, he began reading the Bible every day and paying rapt attention to the messages. Then one day, destiny intervened; Matt and Pam went to church together on a particularly fortuitous day.

The church was a large megachurch in an auditorium-style building. From the moment that a handful of dedicated church members met them at the door, Matt felt welcome. The energy of a live band and a small group of singers, hands in the air, was contagious. When the pastor finally walked out there was first a hush, then a cheer as he praised Jesus. On this particular night, of all nights, the pastor decided to start a series on the importance of

Biblically based relationships. Matt felt as if every word that left the pastor's mouth was directed at him in a mystifying way. Though he knew the message wasn't directed at him, the power of its relevancy settled inside his heart.

"If we're Christians, we need to do the right thing and get married," Matt said weeks later, referring to the way their relationship had grown more serious, and how he was overcome with a desire to change his life according to what he felt was God's plan. In 2007, three years after he'd walked out of prison prepared to start life over again, he and Pam were married in the turn-of-the-century rose garden of a local park.

Matt decided against becoming involved in the prison ministry. Entering the prison, even as a free person, was too daunting. Instead, he began ministering to inmates who'd recently been released and were looking to change their lives. He'd been sharing his faith with Dan and another friend as well, but his words had so far fallen on closed ears. He wanted the same peace for them that he felt. The nightmares he'd suffered for decades had vanished. He was no longer grasping for stability. Now, each Word transformed into another support beam for his structure.

"I feel called to share the Good News, and maybe I'm planting a seed in the same way people planted a seed in my heart at one time," he said to Pam, feeling that no conversation about God was ever a waste of time even if nothing visible came from it. He felt no pressure to find the right words or to hammer away at Dan. He just spoke what was in his heart when the opportunities arose and left the rest to God.

Matt knew his brother so well that he noticed even the smallest changes in Dan. One day he found Dan in a particularly glum mood. There was even a vein popping out on Dan's forehead he'd never seen before. Matt responded with a typical cutting comment to lighten the mood and wasn't prepared for Dan's crushing news.

"I have prostate cancer."

Though he immediately felt in his heart that God was in control, Matt reached out to steady himself, then sat down. The brothers talked about past memories. Matt talked about God. They talked about life in general. Matt poured out his heart about his new life in Christ and read to him Romans 3:23–25.

"For all have sinned and fall short of the glory of God and are justified by his grace as a gift, through the redemption that is in Jesus Christ."

And one day, Dan felt his heart open. The injustices they'd shared at the hands of Tom had gone unspoken between them, so there had never been the opportunity to unburden themselves of those hurts. After forty-seven years of challenges and bickering, the brothers saw eye-to-eye, and Dan accepted Christ.

"The end of this life is closing for you, Dan, but we're finally developing the relationship of brotherly love we were always meant to have. It's never too late." Still tied to the dysfunction that had never quite left their lives, they went through Dan's house, at Matt's request, to rid it of pornography and drug-related items. It was an outer cleansing that followed the inner one. The student had become the teacher. Where once Dan spoke with the wisdom and authority of an older brother, now Matt took the lead. When Dan passed away a year later, he said he could do so with peace in his heart. He had God and knew his son was on the right path.

Wade became a neurological-based chiropractor specializing in the brain and spinal cord. He married a woman who later came to share his passion for Christ and family. They went on to have ten children; five boys and five girls! He continues to practice neurological-based care in Minnesota. People travel hundreds of miles daily and sometimes fly into Minneapolis to receive his powerful method of treatment. "My model of care is uncommon in the fact that I pray with all of my patients and teach them Biblical health principles. I have been blessed to see amazing miracles take place in my clinic and give all the glory to God!" Wade said.

And Matt continues to lead a new life. He now spends his time leisurely riding his motorcycle, having quiet evenings with Mary and Pam, going on walks with his black lab, Willie, and watching classic Billy Graham crusades on television. Since 2004, he has held a steady job, works with those struggling to rebuild their lives, attends church regularly, tithes, and has ceased adding to his rap sheet. Many debts can't be paid back with money but only with actions. Matt felt not only a duty but a desire to give back to those who never abandoned him. When Mary's health declined, he and Pam first moved to be close enough to help care for Mary before moving her into their home. His life didn't transform perfectly overnight.

He began to see the world through new eyes; he made room for love, honesty, trust, and commitment. Matt is proceeding with prayer to get to know his daughter.

"Are you sure you want your life story out there for your daughter to read?" A friend asked this out of concern for Matt.

"It's not who you were; it's who you are," he answered with confidence.

Shortly after leaving prison for the last time, he shared another observation.

"I decided to throw out the bad parts, and when I was done, there were enough good pieces left to make a new creation. I think you'll like the new guy."

Matt and Pam on their wedding day in 2007 in the garden of McKennan Park in Sioux Falls, SD. In spite of all the efforts to leave his former life behind, one dedicated criminal associate showed up uninvited. Matt spotted him sitting on a park bench, with a Pit Bull on its leash, watching the wedding from a distance.

Book Discussion Questions

1. What preconceived opinions did you have about the subject of the story, and did these change after reading the book?

2. Did the author/subject succeed in teaching you anything? If so, what did you take away from the book?

3. What is the religious function of this book? Did you relate to any of the characters' feelings about religion? If so, how?

4. Did you learn anything new about yourself by reading this book? Elaborate.

5. Was there a specific passage or quote from the book that left an impression on you?

6. To what degree, if any, are the various characters innocent? Do you consider any of them to be victims of their circumstances?

7. Making bad choices is a major theme in the book. Matt makes wrong choices that land him in prison. Dan makes wrong choices that result in paralysis. Mary makes the wrong choices with men. What version of this do you see in your own life or in the life of someone close to you?

8. In the book, we see the dynamics between the two brothers. What is each brother's role in the family, and how does this change by the end of the book?

9. Were you surprised by the way Matt's life changed by the end of the book?

10. In your opinion, what was the main message of the book?

About the Authors

PHIL AND SANDY HAMMAN are both teachers in Sioux City, Iowa. They are the authors of the bestseller, *Gitchie Girl*. Phil has also written two memoirs, *Under the Influence* and *disOrder*. The authors speak regularly at churches, schools, and universities. Phil and Sandy have been married since 1984, and Matt Lofton, the subject of *Rap Sheet* was in their wedding in between his many incarcerations.

CPSIA information can be obtained
at www.ICGtesting.com
Printed in the USA
BVOW03s1640051017
496826BV00002B/3/P